Storm for
the Living and
the Dead

also by charles bukowski

The Days Run Away Like Wild Horses Over the Hills (1969)

Post Office (1971)

Mockingbird Wish Me Luck (1972)

South of No North (1973)

Burning in Water, Drowning in Flame: Selected Poems 1955–1973 (1974)

Factotum (1975)

Love Is a Dog from Hell (1977)

Women (1978)

You Kissed Lilly (1978)

Play the Piano Drunk Like a Percussion Instrument Until the Fingers Begin to Bleed a Bit (1979)

Shakespeare Never Did This (1979)

Dangling in the Tournefortia (1981)

Ham on Rye (1982)

Bring Me Your Love (1983)

Hot Water Music (1983)

There's No Business (1984)

War All the Time: Poems 1981–1984 (1984)

You Get So Alone at Times That It Just Makes Sense (1986)

The Movie: "Barfly" (1987)

The Roominghouse Madrigals: Early Selected Poems 1946–1966 (1988)

Hollywood (1989)

Septuagenarian Stew: Stories & Poems (1990)

The Last Night of the Earth Poems (1992)

Screams from the Balcony: Selected Letters 1960–1970 (1993)

Storm for the Living and the Dead

Uncollected and Unpublished Poems

Charles Bukowski

Edited by Abel Debritto

ecco

An Imprint of HarperCollinsPublishers

Art created by Charles Bukowski and is courtesy of Linda Lee Bukowski.

STORM FOR THE LIVING AND THE DEAD. Copyright © 2017 by Linda Lee Bukowski. All rights reserved. Printed in the United States of America. No part of this book may be used or reproduced in any manner whatsoever without written permission except in the case of brief quotations embodied in critical articles and reviews. For information, address HarperCollins Publishers, 195 Broadway, New York, NY 10007.

HarperCollins books may be purchased for educational, business, or sales promotional use. For information, please e-mail the Special Markets Department at SPsales@harpercollins.com.

A hardcover edition of this book was published in 2017 by Ecco, an imprint of HarperCollins Publishers.

FIRST ECCO PAPERBACK EDITION PUBLISHED 2019.

Designed by Renata De Oliveira

Library of Congress Cataloging-in-Publication Data has been applied for.

ISBN 978-0-06-265652-0

23 24 25 26 27 LBC 9 8 7 6 5

Storm for the Living and the Dead

caught again at some impossible pass

and the one with big feet, stupid, would not move
when I passed thro the aisle; that night at the barn
dance Elmer Whitefield lost a tooth fighting big
Eddie Green;
we'll get his radio and we'll get his watch, they said,
pointing at me, damn Yankee; but they didn't know
I was an insane poet and I leaned there drinking wine
and loving all their women
with my eyes, and they were frightened and cowed
as any small town cattle
trying to figure out how to kill me
but first
foolishly
needing a reason; I could have told them
how not so long ago
I had almost killed for lack of reason;
instead, I took the 8:15 bus
to Memphis.

in this—

in this, grows the word of arrow;
we ache all through with simple terror
while walking down a simple street
and see where the tanks have piled it up:
faces run through, apples live with worms
to a squeeze of love; or out there—
where the sailors drowned, and the sea
washed it up, and your dog sniffed
and ran as if his hinds had been bitten
by the devil.

in this, say that Dylan wept
or Ezra crawled with Muss
through thin Italian hours
as my fine brown dog
forgot the devil
or cathedrals shaking in sunlight's gunfire,
and found love easily
upon the street outside.

in this, it's true: that which makes iron
makes roses makes saints makes rapists
makes the decay of a tooth and a nation.

in this, a poem could be absence of word.
the smoke that once came up to push ten tons of steel
now lies flat and silent in an engineer's hand.

in this, I see Brazil in the bottom of my glass.
I see hummingbirds—like flies, dozens of them—
stuck in a golden net. HELL!!—I have *died* in Words
like a man on a narcotic of thinning nectar!

in this, like blue through blue without bacchanalia dreams
where the tanks have piled it up, big boys shoot pool,
elf-eyes through smoke and waiting:
A CRACK AND BALLS, THAT'S ALL, ISN'T IT?

and courses in definitive literature.

why are all your poems personal?

_____

why are all your poems personal? she
said, no wonder she hated you . . .
which one? I said. you know
which one . . . and don't ever leave
water in your sink again, and you
can't broil a roast; my landlady said
you're very handsome and she wanted to
know why we didn't get together
again . . .

did you tell her?

could I tell her you're conceited
and alcoholic? could I tell her about
the time I had to pick you up
off your back
when you had that fight?
could I tell her
you play with yourself?
could I tell her
you think
you're Mr. Vanbilderass?

why don't you go home?

I've always loved you, you know
I've always loved you!

good. some day I'll write a poem about
it. a very personal
poem.

prayer for broken-handed lovers

in dwarfed and towering rage, in ambulances of hate,
stamping out the ants, stamping out the sleepless ants
forevermore . . . pray for my horses, do not pray for me;
pray for the fenders of my car, pray for the carbon on
the filaments of my brain . . . exactly, and listen,
I do not need any more love, any more wet stockings
like legs of death crawling my face in a midnight's
bathroom . . . make me sightless of blood and wisdom and
despair, don't let me see the drying carnation
pinking-out against my time, buttonholed and rootless
as the tombs of memory;
                                          well, I've been bombed out of
better places than this, I've had the sherry shaken
out of my hand, I've seen the teeth of the piano move
filled with explosions of rot; I've seen the rats in
the fireplace
                    leaping like rockets through the flames;
pray for Germany, pray for France, pray for Russia,
do not pray for me . . . and yet . . . and yet I can see again
the crossing of the lovely legs, of more sherry and more
disappointment, more bombs—surging seas of bombs,
my paintings flying like birds amongst the earrings
and bottles, amongst the red lips, amongst the love letters
and the last piano, I will cry that I was right: we
never should have been.

fast pace

I came in awful tired with a finger sliced off and frost
on my feet and the lightning coming down the wallpaper;
they hung three men in the streets and the mayor was drunk
on candy, and they sunk the friggin' fleet and the vultures
were smoking Havana cigars; o.k., I see where some bathing
beauty sliced her left wrist an' they found her in a comatose
state in her bedroom—probably pining her heart out for
me, but I've got to move out of town: I thought I was a
no-sweat kid, a rock, but I just found a

grey hair above my
left ear.

I think of Hemingway

I think of Hemingway sitting
in a chair, he had a typewriter
and now he no longer touches
his typewriter, he has no more
to say.

and now Belmonte has no more
bulls to kill, sometimes I think
I have no more poems to write,
no more women to love.

I think of the form of the poem
but my feet hurt, there is dirt
on the windows.

the bulls sleep nights in the
fields, they sleep good without
Belmonte.

Belmonte sleeps good without
Belmonte but I do not sleep
so well.

I have neither created nor
loved for some time, I swat
at a fly and miss, I am an
old grey dog growing tooth-
less.

I have a typewriter and now
my typewriter no longer has
anything to say.

I will drink until morning
finds me in bed with the
biggest whore of them all:
myself.

Belmonte & Poppa, I under-
stand, this is the way it
goes, truly.

I have watched them bring
the dirt down all morning
to fill the holes in the
streets. I have watched
them put new wires on
the poles, it rained
last night, a very
dry rain, it was
not a bombing, only the
world is ending and I am
unable to write
about it.

A Private Poem, not for publication, as if
publication
at all
mattered,
hail.   I WAS SHIT

CHARLES BUKOWSKI
1623 N. MARIPOSA AVE.
Los Angeles 27, CALIF.

grief, the walls are bloody with grief and who cares?--
a sparrow, a princess, a whore, a bloodhound?
by god, dirt cares, dirt, and dirt I shall be,
I'll score a heroe's blast where heroes are all the same:
Ezra packed next to gopher just as I,
just as I, the faint splash of rain in the empty brain,
o by god, the noble intentions, the lives, the sewers,
the tables in Paris
flaunting and floating in our swine memories,
Havanna, Cuba, Hemingway
falling to the floor
blood splashing all exits.

if Hemingway kills himself
what am I?
if Cummings dies across his typewriter,
if Faulkner clutches his heart and goes,
what am I?
what am I? what was I
when Jeffers died in his tomb,
his stone cocoon.

I was shit, shit, shit, shit.

I now fall to the floor and raise the last of myself
what's left of myself
I promise grails filled with words as well as wine,
and the green, and the shade flapping,
all this is nothing,
God shaving in my bathroom,
rent due,
lightning breaking the backs of ants,
I must close in upon myself,
I must stop playing tricks for
deep inside
somewhere
above the nuts or
below   or in that head
not yet crushed
eyes looking out like damned and impossible fires,
I see the gap I must leap, and I will be strong
and I will be kind, I have always been kind,
animals love me as if I were a child ######### crayoning
the edges of the world,
sparrows walk right by, flies crawl under## my eyelids,
I cannot hurt anything
but myself,
I cannot even in the bloody grief
scream;
this is more than a scripture inside my brain--
I am tossed along the avenues of trail and trial
like dice
the gods mouthing their fires of strength
and I
must not die,   ~~but~~
    yet.

I was shit

grief, the walls are bloody with grief and who cares?
a sparrow, a princess, a whore, a bloodhound?
by god, *dirt* cares, dirt, and dirt I shall be,
I'll score a hero's blast where heroes are all the same:
Ezra packed next to gopher just as I,
just as I, the faint splash of rain in the empty brain,
o by god, the noble intentions, the lives, the sewers,
the tables in Paris
flaunting and floating in our swine memories,
Havana, Cuba, Hemingway
falling to the floor
blood splashing all exits.

if Hemingway kills himself
what am I?
if Cummings dies across his typewriter,
if Faulkner clutches his heart and goes,
what am I?
what am I? what was I
when Jeffers died in his tomb,
his stone cocoon?

I was shit, shit, shit, shit.

I now fall to the floor and raise the last of myself
what's left of myself
I promise grails filled with words as well as wine,
and the green, and the shade flapping,
all this is nothing,
God shaving in my bathroom,
rent due,
lightning breaking the backs of ants,
I must close in upon myself,
I must stop playing tricks for
deep inside
somewhere
above the nuts or
below or in that head
not yet crushed
eyes looking out like damned and impossible fires,
I see the gap I must leap, and I will be strong
and I will be kind, I have always been kind,
animals love me as if I were a child crayoning
the edges of the world,
sparrows walk right by, flies crawl under my eyelids,
I cannot hurt anything
but myself,
I cannot even in the bloody grief
scream;
this is more than a scripture inside my brain—
I am tossed along the avenues of trail and trial
like dice
the gods mouthing their fires of strength
and I
must not die,
yet.

corrections of self, mostly after Whitman:

I would break the boulevards like straws
and put old rattled poets who sip milk
and lift weights
into the drunk tanks from Iowa
to San Diego;
I would announce my own firm intention to immortality
quietly
since nobody would listen anyway,
and I would break the Victrola
I would break the soul of Caruso
on a warm night full of flies;
I would go hymie-ass
shifting it up the boulevards
on an old Italian racing bike,
glancing backwards
always knowing
like goodnights in Germany
or gloves thrown down,
it happens.

I would cry for the armies of Spain,
I would cry for Indians gone to wine,
I would cry, even, for Gable dead
if I could find a tear;

I would write introductions to books of poetry
of young men gone half-daft
with the word;
I would kill an elephant with a bowie knife
to see his trunk fall
like an empty stocking.

I would find things in sand and things
under my bed: teeth-marks, arm-marks, signs,
tips, paint-stains, love-stains, scratchings
of Swinburne . . .

I would break the mountains for their olive pits,
I would keen dead-nosed divers
with ways to go,
and as it happens
I would swat and kill one more fly
or write
one more useless poem.

the bumblebee

she dressed like a bumblebee,
black stripes on yellow,
and *clish clish slitch* went
the gun, the gun was always there,
and those hard things like eyes,
stones in the bottom of a rank pond,
and I met her at *Vince's*
although what we spoke of is
beyond me, and she took me to her
apartment, a very nifty place
with a couple of beds, a waxed
kitchen floor, and a tv walking around
like a tiger, and I dumped the steaks,
the whiskey and the beer on the table,
and later we ate, she made a good salad,
and we had some drinks and watched the
tiger walking and then I killed the thing
and I told the bumblebee that I was dying,
they had taken away my fountains,
that any going on seemed senseless,
drunkenness only evicted me from
one plane of failure to another,
but this she did not understand,
and later on the bed

she climbed upon *me*
this bumblebee
and I clenched the cheeks of her ass
and it was real enough, she had the stinger
turned down, and I said,
beautiful o beautiful
but I could do nothing,
I was dying and she was dead,
and later, dressed again,
I said goodbye at the door,
I said forgive me, and then the door
was closed
and I ran down the halls   I ran
outside for air
those little stone eyes rattling in
my head, and I got into my car
and drove 20 miles south to the beach
and I stood on the pier
and watched the waves,
imagined gigantic sea battles,
I became salt and sand and sound,
and soon the eyes went away
and I lit a cigarette,
coughed, and walked back
toward the car.

warble in

warble in the blackbird of my night
through pitchblende breathing,
and may the counties raise their taxes
and the axman itch in his sleep;
warble in the blackbird of my night,
and may the armies dress for dancing
in the streets, and young girls
kiss the fruits that fill their bellies;
warble in the blackbird of my night,
grunt and groan your Summers down,
pick at lily stems when
cancer's heart burns love;
warble in the blackbird of my night,
warble in the note,
my country's tall for falling
the rust of days
from Moscow to New York
adds a terror of hours
but I do not complain
the ten thousand kisses
or the sticks and stones
or broken Rome,
but I wait your note,
my fingers scratch
this sunlit table.

a trainride in hell

GO GO GO GO GO! they yell
and a monkey reaches up and twists out the light
and the old redhead in the black dress
lifts her skirts and dances
GO GO GO GO GO!
she wiggles her well-done hump of a tail
and then the cop comes in through the vestibule
and they cheer
YAY!!!   YAY!!!
and he moves off with the redhead in front of him
hair in her eyes, mouth twisted down in disgust,
and they scream at him,
YOU TAKE IT! HAVE A NICE PIECE!   YAY!!!!

it is a trainride in hell,
the losers from the racetrack going one hundred miles home
to jobs and no jobs, wives and no wives, lives and no lives,
and the jack behind the bar has only beer,
it floats in a trashcan of ice and he dumps the hot beer in—
(YAY!!!!   YAY!! they scream every time a new person enters the barcar)
and grabs cans and opens and sells them as fast as the machine
will punch holes . . .
GO GO GO GO GO GO!!! they have found a new one
and she dances (the whores get on at San Clemente
where they have been sitting in the bars

and they ride north to L.A.
picking up what they can)
and now she is rolling imaginary dice,
no, they are real, there are quarters on the floor,
she wiggles the dice, she wiggles her can and they scream
GO GO GO GO GO!!!

the cop comes through again and the dice disappear,
he is smoking a cigarette and his cap is pushed back,
he is grey and looks more drunkard than any of us,
YAY!! YAY! they cheer him, and he walks on.

an extrovert in a blue sports shirt
moves around hugging and kissing the women,
then a colored girl hangs from her knees from a crossbar,
YAY! GO GO GO! YAY!

a homosexual pushes his face in mine,
"have you been to the racetrack?"
I move away from him, walk to the bar and
sweat my wait for a beer.

YAY! GO GO GO GO!

the colored girl dances opposite a chinaman,
GO GO GO GO!

I get my beer.

outside, the buildings go by, people looking at television,
in Berlin they fuck with their wall,
people ponder issues of state with stones,

here an old blond presses her flank against mine,
I buy her a beer and a pack of Pall Malls,
then she says, "come with me, I have to go to the can,"
and we walk past the crowd,
YAY! YAY!   THERE THEY GO! GO GO GO GO!!!

she is wearing slacks and her belly presses out from the top
of them, and I wait outside the sign that says WOMEN,
and I am sweating and impatient for the little the beer is doing
and I empty the can and throw it in the vestibule
and I drink hers too, and in the other car
the people are tired and miserable, re-dreaming their losses,
strung out in their seats, stuffed things,
taken—again—by the world,

and my whore comes out
and we walk again into the barcar,
yay! YAY!   GO GO GO GO!
DANCE, DANCE, DANCE!
and she begins to dance wobbling what is left of the
masquerade of her flesh and I leave her and go to the bar,
GO   GO GO GO   GO GO   GO GO GO!

there is still beer left, the jack is dragging it out of closets,
the train sways sways doing 90   95   98
the engineer a loser too
popping a keg of beer between his legs,
and I think of the battles fought through the centuries,
the battles in small rooms, on battlefields,
madman, genius, idiot, fake,
all drawing blood, all wasted, wasted, wasted,
the roaches will crawl everywhere
over Schubert's Symphony #9,

in and out of our ears
GO GO GO GO GO!!!
and yet here
this too
means something

and my whore is back and we drink
until some crazy jack turns on the fire system
and the lights go out
and we are all under a cold shower
yay! YAY!   GO GO GO GO GO GO GO!

somebody gets the water off, and the lights on
and the women all have toadsheads
the hair flat, mascara gone, eyelids gone, and they are giggling,
purses and mirrors out, combs out, trying to hide from life again,
and I look away, cool at last, get a couple more beers,
find a dry cigarette and light up,
and then like another sore
Los Angeles is upon us
and we are out of the doors
running down the ramps
YAY!   GO, GO, GO, GO!

there is a wheelchair in the aisle,
and the extrovert in the blue sports shirt
puts his friend in it,
SICK MAN! SICK MAN! GANGWAY!
HEY GANGWAY! DYING MAN!

they move at a very rapid speed
to put it blandly, HEY! GANGWAY! SICK MAN!

oh, GO GO GO GO GO GO!
oh, GO GO GO   GO, GO, GO!   YAYY!!

a guard stops them and takes the wheelchair
and then my friend in the blue shirt
picks his friend up and puts him over his shoulder
and hurries down the ramp,
HEY! HEY! GANGWAY, DYING MAN!

my whore is still there when I get to my car
in the parking lot, she gets in
and we drive off past the city hall
and onto the freeway, and there is one more race
to be run without a winner, and all around us drive
people who have been to the baseball game
or the beach or a movie or Aunt Sarah's,
and the whore says, "that Marmatz. I just don't know.
the kid won't win for me."

20 minutes later she is in my room.

GO, GO, GO, GO, GO, GO!

                    yay.

outside it is very still, and you can hear the bombers overhead,
you can hear the mice making love; you can hear them digging
the graves at the cemeteries, you can hear worms crawling into
sockets, and the train we came in on, it sits very still now,
it is quiet, the windows show nothing but moonlight,
there is a sadness like old rivers, and it is more real
than it has ever been.

same old thing, Shakespeare
through Mailer—

into all instants before we like
woodchoppers die I would like to
think that what we've said will
not necessarily follow us into
that dark hole that is not love
or sex or anything we know now,
and when the troops marched into
Turkey they ran through the first
village raping the young girls
and some of the old ones too,
and Anderson and I found a café
and sat there drinking listening
to the air-arm overhead sinking
in its fangs and I said it's the
same old thing Shakespeare through
Mailer sticking his wife with the
same thing but the wrong thing,
and I thought if we could die here
now in a minute like a camera
snapped it would be much best
all the mules and drunken ladies
gone   the bad novels   march
stuck in the mud   it is best

to die when you are ready
like razorblades and beer-songs
to an ancient Irish tune
and then some Turk took a shot
from the staircase and split my
sleeve like a tight ass bending
and I fired back like people in
a play and I kept thinking
Maria Maria I wonder if I'll
ever see Maria again, and
immortality did not seem
important at all.

the rope of glass

the old man was older than I
on the train going south
along the sea there
then the train ran
in between yellow cliffs and
the sea was shut off and
he told me,

> "in 1914 I took 400 mules
> from Missouri to Italy.
> those mules stank.
> it took more than one boat
> but I got 'em there.
> they used the mules to
> haul cannon up the mountain.
> the Austrians and the Italians
> fought the whole war over
> one mountain."

the train came out from between the
cliffs, and down in the sea
the swimmers swam
boys came in like madness
on surfboards. I had been reading
the *Racing Form*.

"we made bridges of rope from
mountain to mountain
always going up
and the mules pulled the cannon
across."

"bridges of rope?" I
asked.

"this was glass rope, nothing
stronger, we tightened the works
with a wheel like a molasses wheel
and the mule and cannon went across.
there was no air power then and
when we got the cannon to the top
we pointed them down and
shelled the city below
us."

I left him when the train reached the
track, he was an old man
looking out of a window.
I walked across the bridge, a wooden one,
over inland seawater that
smelled of rot. I walked toward the
track, it was hot, it was a Saturday in
August 1964 and the world
was still
fighting.

tough luck

good things are around if you
search them out.
I remember this time in the German prison camp
we got holda this queer
they come in handy in times of no women
and we beat the shit outa him first
and then we passed him around
and we had him sucking one guy's dick
while the other guy reamed him
and even one of the German guards came in
and took some—what a night!
and that queer couldn't walk for a month
and he got shot and killed one night
trying to bust through the wire
and I remember Harry moaning
as they took the fag past
with those 2 holes in his head:
"there goes the best piece I ever
had!"

sometimes when I feel blue
I listen to Mahler

no cream job, Harry,
some hairy Moses like me is just dragging for shelter now
like a picture of St. Louis in the snow, but, no, it's hot:
enough oil for the fan, and
too lazy to change the dirty sheets,
too crazy to care.

I used to write mother about razorblades against my throat
about how awful faces on people looked
how their bodies were like hardened tar
but dear old mama died of cancer while I was lying with
a 300-pound whore who swam in all the way from
Costa Rica
and I had to get a job in the railroad yards,
shit yeah, and I keep thinking that the last razor against my throat
will understand the divinity of steel and
the undivinity of
waiting.

I haven't written, Harry, no cream,
because I've got this place in the back, I mean there's a
back window to this room
and I look out and there's this woman always hanging washing

about 35
and when she bends over to get her panties and bras and bedsheets
and nylons from the basket,
ah—
it's all there, Harry,
and I'm *looking*
EYES LEAPING THROUGH THE DIRTY WINDOWPANES
and I'm like a pimply high-school kid again
never had a piece of ass like that,
here she is in starched gingham,
red and white squares
and that ass big as the Empire State Building
looking me in the mouth
and the sun coming down on everything
and in the corner of my room
a square of melting butter in a dish
a piece of dry bread
and a spider in the corner
sucking Pepsi-Cola from a fly—
cream, Harry, CREAM!
                    and
sometimes when I get blue I listen to Mahler
or read a little Artaud
or I go out in the yard where they have this turtle
and when nobody is looking
I burn his neck with my cigar
and when the head goes in the shell I poke the cigar in
the hole like a hot
dick, but you know, really, there's nothing being written,
yet I keep getting these rejects,
I write good stuff too, Harry, no cream—
true genius just usually isn't recognized in a

lifetime
and so I am not discouraged—
right now I am listening to "The March of the Smugglers"
from the Carmen Suite by Bizet,
what terrible dripping shit,
I think I'll try that monkey Malone
at *Wormwood*—he prints Bukowski
so he'll print anybody. by the way, Bukowski lives in the room
across the hall,
a jerk, the other day we are all at Dirty Jane's room,
we're drinking port wine
and Bukowski snatches Dirty Jane's drawers right off
and goes to it
right in front of
everybody. I mean, he ate
it. if he can do it
I can do it too. and he had the nerve to tell me,
"the next time I see you burn that turtle
I am going to kill you!"
and he was so drunk I could have knocked him down with a
flyswatter.
              no cream job, Harry, I haven't written in months
but the next thing I write has got to
go, I can feel the swelling in me like the quills on a cat's cock
jammed in a turkey's ass.
the sun is raiding my temples
and the wallpaper dances with naked girls after one
A.M.
I see finer and finer ways of shooting a solid line to
the moon,   no shit, boy, this is
it, the typewriter is my machinegun
and RIP TAP TAP TAP RIP

ALL THE SKY WILL FALL   and beautiful girls
with eyes like bursting heaven
will hold my banana; everything is here—
the waste of sewers, the dull mountains,
equity,
1690 cubic feet, anorexia, the shade of
Marcus Junius Brutus &
a new typewriter ribbon.
a photo of Hemingway pasted in my
bathroom.

god christ, Harry, I am a writer,
and it's not easy when I am the only one who knows it,
except maybe Dirty Jane,
but I'll probably end up some day so famous
that I won't be able to stand myself
and it will be the razor.
anyhow, strange ending
to the same dirty game.
                Bukowski just by to borrow a razorblade—
wonder what he needs it for
with all that
beard?

men's crapper

take this one:
first before he shits he wipes with
easy grace the
lid of the seat, he really *shines* the damn
thing
then he spreads toilet paper over the seat,
quite neatly, even
dangling a gob of it where his powerful genitals will
hang, and then he lowers with
dignity and manliness
his shorts and pants
and
    sits and
          shits
almost without *passion*
scuffling an old dirty newspaper
between his feet and reading about yesterday's basketball
game—
this you see here is a Man: worldly, and no crabs for this
baby, and an easy
a real easy
shit, and he will wipe his ass
while conversing with the man who is washing his hands
at the nearest sink,

and if you are standing nearby
his little mouse eyes will fall upon yours without a
quiver, and then—
the shorts up, the pants up, the hook of belt, the flush of
toilet,
the washing of the hands
and then he stands before the mirror
surveying the glory of himself
combing his hair carefully in neat and
delicate swoops, finishing,
then putting that
face
close to the mirror
and looking in and upon himself, then
satisfied
he leaves
first making sure to give you the elbow
or the ponderous nightmare insult of his empty
eyes, and then with
the twirling of his dumbstruck egotistical buttocks
he leaves the men's room,
and I am left with facetowels like flowers
mirrors like the sea
and I am left with the sickest of hopes
that someday the real human being will arrive
so that there will be something to save
let alone
shit
out.

like a flyswatter

write to the president
it is coming through
everything is coming through

some day you will kiss dogs on the street
some day all the money that you will need will be
yourself

it will be so easy that we will go completely or
seemingly mad and
sing for hours
making up words and laughing

sweet jesus boy
the dream is so near
you can touch it like a
flyswatter
while working through walls toward
burial

the Bomb itself won't matter
peanut butter bluebirds torn before your eyes won't
matter

it is just
the conformation of light and idea and stride all
bunched
ganged
walking along

a hell of a mighty night
a hell of a mighty way

it's so easy

some day I will walk into a cage with a bear
sit down and light a cigarette
look at Him
and He will sit down and cry,
40 billion people watching without sound
as the sky turns upside down and
splits the backbone
open.

take me out to the ball game

the girls can take it
sideways
standing up
or upside down on their heads
or on your
head

how the girls can take it
front or
back
bite
suck
tongue
leather
slap
punch
knife
burn
tanned or bathed in orgy butter

drunk
sober
high
angry

vicious
happy
pretending

the girls can take it
all you've
got and room for
more;
what little you've
got—
penis, heart, lungbreath, sweatstink
albatross moan
elephant insight
flea scream

warty hogtongued old men
young boys with sad pimples

madman and genius

butchers and nazis
sadists and simpletons

gas men
ass men
half-men
elf-men

bellboys—

how the girls can take it,
you can drive a Helm's Bakery truck through it
whistle blowing

you can play a harmonica with it,
make men jump bridges for it
or because of it
or because of it not,

but it just isn't all that good
farting
legs back in ridiculous supine position,
it's a kind of a cunty trick to chop the blueness out of your
eyes
to boggle your ass like a looney
praying for ejaculation proof
of some pre-created
cardboard
schoolboy Manhood.

the girls can take it
will take it
can take you
make you into a Captain of Industry or
an eater of shit,
anything they want

they can bury you, marry you
flog you
cover you with icing like a cake
put your dick into a jar of black widow spiders
and make you sing
TAKE ME OUT TO THE BALL GAME!
the girls walking along on Sunday mornings
can make you think of Mahler
the paintings of Cézanne

they can make you think of quiet things
quiet true and easy
things;
how they sway and glide in their yellow and
blue dresses . . .

they've put half the madmen beating their padded walls
where they are, god,
I once chased one half across the state of Nevada
and when I spun her around
I saw I had been chasing the same ass
but it was upon the body of another woman!

I've cleaned out entire bars in my fury,
tried to drown myself
in dirty apartment house bathtubs,
and for what?—
a cunt.
a hole in the wall.
a mirage.
cheese on the windowsill
covered with flies.

how the girls can take it.
how the girls can bring it on.
keep it going.
the Soviet tanks rolled into Prague today
filled with their children.

the girls wear flowers in their hair.
I love them.

I thought I was going to get some

I had just vomited out the door of my car
had mixed reds, wine, beer and whiskey.
late Saturday night
no, early Sunday morning;
I couldn't take much more; I was always
killing myself
ending up in jails, hospitals, doorways, floors . . .
translated into 7 languages
taught in half a dozen modern lit. courses,
I still didn't know anything,
didn't want to;
I finished the last retch
closed the door
and swung east on Sunset—
when I saw this thing with long blonde hair
vomiting, really letting it
go—spitting out the rotten life the rotten booze—
the slacks were down, dragging,
ass-bare under the cardboard Hollywood moon—
the thing was really sick:
it heaved, then moved down a little ways,
heaved, all that white ass,
and I thought, shit, I'm gonna get me some—
it's been about 2 years and I'm tired of writing about

hand-jobs—
but when I got up close
I saw that they weren't slacks but pants;
it was just a long-haired kid with a big naked ass,
but then, like my buddy Benny used to say—
"what the hell difference does it make?"
and I was just about to pull over by him
when the squad car saw him
and cut in between us
and the two cops leaped out
quite happy and excited with their find—
"HEY, MOTHER, WHAT YOU DOING WITH YOUR BUNGHOLE
                                          SHOWING?"

the kid spread his legs, threw his arms up into the air.
"HEY, YOU!" one of the cops yelled at me.
I cut my lights and slowly moved on out as if I hadn't
heard. then put it to the floorboard at the first
right. at Gramercy Place and Hollywood Blvd. I stopped
opened the door and
vomited again.

poor son of a bitch, I thought, instead of
taking him home or to a hospital
they'll take him to jail—all that white ass.
maybe they'll take some of it. well, it was too late for
me.

I closed the door, turned on the lights, drove on,
trying to remember where I
lived.

charity ward

and they threw me in a cellar for 3 days
and it was a very dark place, and it seemed as if
everybody were insane down there and that,
at least, kept me happy. but every now and then
a big bastard who called himself
"Booboo Cullers, the big man of the Avenues!"
would come around, I mean he would get out of his bed
and he was huge and mad and I was weak, very,
and he would beat the other patients with his fists,
but I'd always manage to bluff him
I'd pick up my water pitcher
raise back left-handed, curse, and aim.
Boo gave off.

after carrying off 6 dead
one by natural causes
5 by the hands of the wondrous Booboo Cullers
the big man of the Avenues,
they strapped down the huge Booboo
with great difficulty,
and I watched while the wards beat against his
face and his belly and his genitals until he
stopped screaming and subsided
and I smiled and realized that the word
Humanism meant
only the most comfort for the most humans,
which I thought was
very nice.

like that

one of the most beautiful blondes of the screen
unbelievable breasts hips legs waist
everything,
in that car crash
it took her head right off her
body—
like that—
there was her head rolling along the side of
the road,
lipstick on, eyebrows plucked, suntan powder on,
bandanna around hair, it rolled along
like a beach-ball
and the body sat in the car
with those breasts hips legs waist,
everything,
and in the mortuary they put her together again,
sewed the head back
on,
jesus christ, said the guy with the thread,
what a waste.
then he went out and had a hamburger, french fries
and 2 cups of coffee,
black.

phone call from my 5-year-old daughter in Garden Grove

hi, Hank!
I'm still climbing the tree and I haven't fallen
out, so I guess I'll never fall out
now . . .
tuesday night! mama, mama, Hank's coming to see us
tuesday night! can we sleep together, Hank?
that's nice. and we can play in the sandbox before
dinner.
you know, we cleaned it out, Granny and mama and me,
we hosed all these spiders out and we
cleaned the awning. there's only one place where it's
all fucked-up . . . what? I said, "there's only one place
where it's all fucked-up"
it's down in the corner
and you and I can dig that
goop outa
there . . .

the solar mass: soul:
genesis and geotropism:

now let me attempt to
attenuate Veechy's larynx greatness:
for what man of the time could have
said:
"Spooks, Sparks, Spindels—stern strapsin.
Goad oospore from the opine ophite."
Stithy!
and this was before
Pound, Olson, Williams, John
Muir.
"Plan planifolious planimeters!" he once wrote to
me.
"By the beard of the quinquangular rock," I rejoined
him, "you've struck it!"
I visited him in Italy on All Fools' Day
and his mastery of the punctate pulvilli
never left me in doubt
drear.
"Trepan," he said, "ode—whist!—attar astragals."

it was the last. I saw. of him. Veechy had
emblazoned embouchures, cryptonyms, drosometers;
let the favose favor of him
ring through the ruck,
rubefacient, and give too, rustle in the
rutabaga.

hooked on horse

we used to work on stools next to each other.
he was black and I was white
but this isn't a racial thing—
we were horseplaying buddies
and we'd sit there sticking letters
all night and through overtime.
our eyes looked like junkies' eyes:
we were hooked on Horse.
about 2 A.M. I would leap up and throw all my letters down,
"o, jesus!" I'd yell, "o, jesus christ!"
"what what?" my buddy would ask.
I'd stand there with a cigarette burning my lips:
"o, sweet jesus, I've got it! I've got it! o, sweet jesus,
it's so simple! it just came to me! why didn't I think of it?"
"what is it?" he would ask, "tell me."
then the supervisor would run up:
"Bukowski, what the hell's wrong with you? man your case! have

                                                              you
gone crazy?"
I'd stand there and calmly light a new cigarette:
"look, baby, stand off! you bug me! let me be the first to tell you,

                                                          baby,
my working days here are definitely limited! I've got it! I've really

                                                          got it
now!"

"your working days here, Bukowski, are definitely limited! now
                                        man your case and
stop screaming!"
I'd look at him like a dog turd and walk down to the
crapper. why hadn't I thought of it before? I'd buy a place in the
                                        Hollywood
Hills, drink and screw all night, gamble all
day.
then I'd walk back, feeling calm.
it would be all right until 4 A.M. and then my buddy would leap up
throwing his mail all over the case:
"it's all over! it's all over! I've got it! o, my god, I've got it!
it's so simple! all ya gotta do is take the horse that . . ."
"yes, yes?" I'd ask.
and the supervisor would come running down again
and ask my buddy:
"now what the hell's wrong with you? you crazy too?"
"look, man, back off! get your face out of my face
before I cut you loose!"
"you threatenin' me, man?"
"I'm tellin' you, I'm through with this job! now back
off!"

we'd run to the track the next day to make our kill
but that night we'd be back on our postal stools, as
usual. of course, it doesn't make much sense to work for 20 or 30
                                        bucks a night
when you lose 50 bucks a day. he quit first and I soon
followed. I see him at the track every day now.
his wife takes care of him. "I finally got my play straightened out,"
                                        he tells me.

"sure," I say and walk off, thinking, that son of a bitch is *really* crazy,
then I walk toward the 5 win window to place a bet on my newest
angle play,
all you do is take the speed rating, add it to the first 2 figures
in the money
earned column, then you . . .

fuck

fuck the censors
and fuck squiggly joe
and fuck fuck
and fuck you
and fuck me
and fuck the blueberry bush
and a jar of mayonnaise
and fuck the refrigerator
and the priest
and the 3 teeth of the last nun
and fuck the bathtub
and fuck the faucets
and fuck my beerbottle
(but be careful)

fuck the spiral
and the smog
and the pavements
and the calendars
and the poets and the bishops and the kings and
the presidents and the mayors and the councilmen
and the firemen and the policemen
and the magazines and the newspapers and the brown
paper bags

and the stinking sea
and the rising prices and the unemployed
and rope ladders
and gall bladders
and sniffy doctors and orderlies and nice
nurses

and fuck the entire thing,
you know.

do your job.

take it out
and begin.

2 immortal poems

about 2 immortal poems a night
are about all I'll allow myself
to write.
it's fair—there isn't much
competition.
besides, it's more enjoyable
getting drunk
than lasting
forever.

that's why more people
buy liquor than
Shakespeare . . .

who *wouldn't* rather learn to
escape through the neck of a
bottle
or a neatly-rolled
Zig-Zag
than a book?

2 immortal poems a night are
enough . . .
when I hear those high heels

clicking up my doorway
steps . . .
I know that life is not made of paper
and immortality
but what we are
now; and as
her body, her eyes, her soul
enter the
room

the typewriter sits like a spoiled and
wasted, most well-fed
dog . . .

we embrace
within the tiny flash
of our
lives

as the typewriter
yowls
silently.

T.H.I.A.L.H.

in dwarf-like piety the guns mount toward home,
and the coffee cans desire 18th-century verse;
the tabloid is grim with comic strips and
baseball box scores—
as the Egyptians spit on dogs and the geek
swallows lightbulbs at The Metropolitan Museum of
Art; it's haversack and ballyhoo,
the punctuation is regular
the flax is battleship sick
and Captain Claypool vomits midnights out
cleanly;
the destination is the shoebox and the prize is
century-old
taffy, and nobody says
that the purple and green animals
out back by the garbage cans will
control which way the steam will
blow;
pictures of Dempsey and Tunney
crawl across the brain like
snails; and ether is the smell of your dead
psyche;
then, this must be it:
taking your shoes off

across sick evenings
allows ventures that would rip the skull like a
lion's tooth, and Mrs. Carson McCullers is
long dead now
of
drink and
greatness, and the heart still sails like a
boomerang.

the lesbian

(dedicated to all of them)

I was sitting on my couch one night,
as per custom, in shorts and undershirt,
drinking beer and not thinking about too much
when there was a knock on the door—

"woo hooo! woo hooo!"

now what the hell? I thought.

"woo hooo! wooo hooo!"

"what is it?" I asked.

"I got a slim one! I got a slim one for you!"

a slim one?
it sounded like a woman's voice.

"wait a minute," I asked.

I went into the bedroom, put on a ripped shirt and
my dirty chino trousers. then I came out and opened the
door.

it was the lesbian from the place in back.

"I bought a slim one for you," she said.

"oh yeah?"

she was in a tight sweater and shorts,
she turned in the moonlight.

"see? I lost 20 pounds! you like it?"

"come on in," I said.

she sat in the chair across from me and
crossed her legs.

"don't tell the landlady I came by."

"don't worry," I said.

and she crossed her legs the other way. they had
these big purple bruises all over them. I wondered who
had put them there.

she talked and asked questions, talked and asked questions—
who was that woman who came by with the little girl? my little girl,
                                                    was it
my little girl? yes, but they didn't live here. my, that's nice.
her father supported her, her father gave her lots of money, her
                                                    father was a
nice man. was that my painting on the wall? yes, it was. she knew
                                        something about

Art—she said. did I have a girlfriend? what did I do when I wasn't
                                                        sleeping?
she talked and asked questions, talked and asked questions. I was
                                                        bored,
completely out of it.

when I had been a young man
I had thought I could alter nature,
but one lesbian had been simply wood—
wood with a knothole—
and the other
(I tried it twice)
had almost killed me,
chasing me down three flights of steps and
halfway down
Bunker Hill.

the one across from me stood up
walked over, then stuck her breasts in my
face—

"you don't want any, do you?"

"uuh uuh."

she pointed over to a potty chair in the corner—

"you still use that?"

"ah yes. it pinches my cheeks a bit but it brings back
memories . . ."

"good night!" she ran to the door, opened it, slammed
it.

"good night," I
said, and then finished my bottle of beer, thinking,
I wonder what's wrong with
her tonight?

*

then there was a man with little tiny legs running back
there. he had this long body, and these little tiny legs
began where an ordinary man's knees would be
and he ran along with these little tiny legs
packing baskets of food to the lesbian in back there.

my my, there's something wrong with that poor little fellow,
I thought.

the landlord ran him out of there one morning at 5 A.M.

"hey! what the hell you doing up there? get the hell out of
here!"

"I brought her food! I brought her food!"

"get the hell out of here!"

the landlord chased him up the driveway. "you're up there every
damn
morning at 3 A.M. I'm getting sick of it! don't you ever sleep?
what the hell's wrong with your legs?"

"I sleep! I sleep! I work nights!"

they came running past my window.

"you work nights? what the hell's the matter with you? why don't
                                        you get a job
working days?"

little legs just kept running. he made a quick turn around a hedge
                                        and was up the
street. the landlord screamed after him:

"you damn fool! don't you know she's a dyke? what the hell you
                                        gonna do with a
dyke?"

there was no answer, of
course.

                                        *

then the fellow in the next court, a chap a bit on the subnormal
side inherited 20 thousand
dollars. next thing I knew, I heard the lesbian's voice
in there. the walls were quite thin.

god, she got down on her knees and scrubbed all the
floors. and kept running out the back door with the
trash. he musta had a year's worth of trash in
there. each time she ran out the back, the screen door would
slam—bam! bam! bam! it must have slammed 70 times in an
hour and a half. she was showing him.

my bedroom was next to theirs. at night I'd hear him mount
her. there wasn't much action. quite dead. only one body in
motion. your guess.

a few days later the lesbian started to take over—
coming in from the kitchen—
"oh no, buster! get up! get up! you can't go to bed this time
of day! I'm not going to make your bed twice!"

then a week later it was over. I didn't hear her voice anymore.
she was again in her place in the back.

I was standing on my porch one day thinking about it—
poor thing. why doesn't she get a girlfriend? I'm not prejudiced, I
don't hold anything against lesbians, no sir! Look at Sappho. I
                                                        didn't
hold anything against Sappho
either.

then I looked up and here she came down the
driveway. it was too late to run into my
place. I stood quietly, trying to be part of the porch.
she came by in her white shorts and neck bent like a vulture and
then she saw me and made this incredible sound:
"YAWK!"

"good morning," I said.

"YAWK!" she went again.

god damn, I thought, she thinks I'm a bird. I walked quickly into
                                                        my place and

closed the door, looked through the
curtains. she was out there breathing
heavily. then she began to flail her arms up and down, going
"YAWK! YAWK! YAWK!"

she's gone nuts, I
thought.

then slowly slowly she began to rise into the
air.

oh no, I thought.

she was about 3 feet above the hedge,
flailing the air—her breasts bouncing sadly,
her giant legs kicking
looking for notches in the
air. then she rose, higher and
higher. she was above the apartment houses, rising up
into the Los Angeles smog. then she was over Sunset Boulevard
high above the Crocker-Citizens Bank, and
then I saw another object come flying from the
south. it seemed to be all body with just these little short legs
at the back. then they flew toward
each other. when I saw them embrace in mid-air
I turned away, walked into the kitchen and
pulled down all the
shades.
and waited for the end of the
world.
my head rang like a bell
and I began to weep.

a poem to myself

Charles Bukowski   disputes the indisputable
     used to work in the Post Office
     scares people on the streets
     is a neurotic
     makes his shit up
especially the stuff about sex

Charles Bukowski   is the King of the Hard-Mouthed Poets
Charles Bukowski   used to work for the Post Office
Charles Bukowski   writes tough and acts scared
     acts scared and writes tough
     makes his shit up
especially the stuff about sex

Charles Bukowski   has $90,000 in the bank and is
     worried
Charles Bukowski   will make $20,000 a year for the
next 4 years and

     is worried

Charles Bukowski   is a drunk
Charles Bukowski   loves his daughter

| Charles Bukowski | used to work for the Post Office |

Charles Bukowski	says he hates poetry readings
Charles Bukowski	gives poetry readings
	and bitches when the take is under
	$50

Charles Bukowski	got a good review in *Der Spiegel*
Charles Bukowski	was published in Penguin Poetry Series #13
Charles Bukowski	has just written his first novel
	has two old pair of shoes—one black, one
	brown
Charles Bukowski	was once married to a millionairess
Charles Bukowski	is known throughout the underground

Charles Bukowski	sleeps until noon and always awakens with a
	hangover
Charles Bukowski	has been praised by Genet and Henry Miller
	many rich and successful people wish they
	were
Charles Bukowski	

Charles Bukowski	drinks and talks with fascists, revolutionaries,
	cocksuckers, whores and madmen
Charles Bukowski	dislikes poetry
	looks like a fighter but gets beat-up every time
	he drinks scotch or wine

| Charles Bukowski | was a clerk in the Post Office for eleven years |

Charles Bukowski   was a carrier in the Post Office for 3 years
                        wrote *Notes of a Dirty Old Man*
                        which is in bookstores from the Panama
                                                        Canal to
                        Amsterdam

Charles Bukowski   gets drunk with college professors and tells
                                                        them
                        to suck shit;
                        once drank a pint of whiskey straight down
                                                        at a party
                        for squares, and what was
Charles Bukowski   doing there?

Charles Bukowski   is in the archives at the University of Santa
                                                        Barbara
                        that's what started all the riots at Isla Vista

Charles Bukowski   got it made—he can fuck a skunk in a
                                                        cesspool
                        and come up with a royal flush in a Texas
                                                        tornado

                        almost everybody wants to be
Charles Bukowski
                        to get drunk with
Charles Bukowski
                        all the raven-haired girls with tight pussies
                                                        want to
                        fuck

Charles Bukowski

                    even when he speaks of suicide
Charles Bukowski   smiles and sometimes laughs

                    and when his publishers tell him
                    we've hardly made the advance yet
                    or we haven't made our bi-yearly tabulation
                    but you've got it made
Charles Bukowski

                    don't worry

                    and Penguin Books bills
Charles Bukowski   for 2 pounds owed after
                    the first edition has sold out, but don't worry,
                                                    we're
                    going into a second
                    edition,
                    and when the wino on the couch falls on his
                                                    face
                    and Charles Bukowski tries to lift him to the
                                                    couch
                    the wino punches him in the nose

Charles Bukowski   has even had a bibliography written about
                                                    him
                    or tabulated about him
                    he can't miss
                    his piss doesn't stink
                    everything's fine,
                    he even gets drunk with his landlord and
                    landlady, everybody likes him, think he's
                    just just just . . .

Charles Bukowski's   shoulders slump
he pecks at keys that won't answer the call
knowing he's got it made
knowing he's great
Charles Bukowski   is growing broke
is breaking
in a period of acclaim
in a period of professors and publishers and
                                          pussy
nobody will understand that the last of his
                                      bankroll
is burning faster than
dog turds soaked and lit with F-310 gasoline
and Marina needs new
shoes.
of course, he doesn't understand the
intangibles. but he
does.

Charles Bukowski   doesn't have it
he leans across a typewriter
drunk at 3:30 in the morning
let somebody else carry the ball
he's bruised and his ass has been
kicked

it's quits
the night is showing

Charles Bukowski,   dear boy,
                      the game is ending and you
                      never got
                      past midfield,
                      punk.

fact

I have 90 thousand dollars
in the bank
am 50 years old
weigh 280 pounds
never awaken to an alarm clock
and am closer to God
than the
sparrow.

blues song

pardon the territory of my grieving—
it's improper I know,
maybe even
hostile

but the bacon's burning
the bacon's burning

tall nights
armed with machineguns
circle my dizzy and cowardly
bed

the
bacon's
burning

so let's wipe our silly
arses
pretend that we are pleasurable
meaningful things

isn't that the tune
to try to beat
the dirtiest trick of them
all?

fat upon the land

all these,
fat upon the land
teaching English at the universities
and writing
legless
headless
bellybuttonless
poetry

knowing where to apply for the
grants and
getting the grants and
more grants
and writing more
handless
hairless
eyeless
poetry

all these,
fat upon the land
have found a hiding place
and have even achieved wives to
attach to their ninny
souls

72

these,
take paid trips
to the islands
to Europe
Paris
anywhere
in order
it is said
to gather
material
(Mexico, they simply run to on their
own)

while the jails are overcrowded with the
mislaid innocent
while the hunkies go down
in the mines
while idiot sons of the poor
are fired from jobs
these
wouldn't dirty their hands and
souls on

these,
fat upon the land
join at the universities
read their poems to
each other
read their poems to
their students

these,
pretend wisdom and
immortality

control the presses

fat upon the land
as the jail-lines form for half-dinners
while 34 hunkies are trapped in a
mine

these

board a boat for a south sea island
to gather an anthologized
poetry of
friends

and/or

appear at anti-war demonstrations
without ever knowing what
any kind of war
is

fat upon the land
they are drawing a map of our
culture—
a division of zero,
a multiplication of
senseless
grace

"Robert Hunkerford teaches English at
S.U. Married. 2 children, pet dog.
This is his first collection of

verse. He is presently working on a
translation of the poems of
Vallejo. Mr. Hunkerford was awarded
a Sol Stein last year."

these,
fat upon the land
teaching English at the universities
and writing
neckless
handless
ball-less
poetry

such is the manner and the way
and why the people
do not understand
the streets
the verse
the war
or
their hands upon the
table

our culture is hiding in the lace dreams of
our English classes
in the lace dresses of our English
classes

American classes
is what we need
and American poets

from mines
the docks
the factories
the jails
the hospitals
the bars
the ships
the steel mills.
American poets,
deserters from armies
deserters from madhouses
deserters from strangling wives and lives;
American poets:
ice cream-men, necktie-salesmen, corner paperboys,
warehousemen, stockboys, messengerboys,
pimps, elevator operators, plumbers, dentists, clowns, hot-
walkers, jockeys, murderers (we've been hearing from the
murdered), barbers, mechanics, waiters, bellboys,
dope-runners, boxers, bartenders, others others
others

until these arrive
our land will remain
dead and ashamed

the head guillotined off
and speaking to the students
in English II

this is your culture
but not
mine.

love song

I have eaten your cunt like a peach,
I have swallowed the seed
the fuzz,
locked in your legs
I have sucked and chewed and tongued and
swallowed you,
have felt your whole body jerk and twist as
one
machinegunned
and I made my tongue into a point
and the juices slid down
and I swallowed
maddened
and sucked your whole insides out—
your entire cunt sucked into my mouth
I bit
I bit
and swallowed
and you too
went mad
and I drew away and kissed
then your belly
your bellybutton
then slid down inside your white flower legs

and kissed and bit and
nibbled,
all the time
once again
those wondrous cunt hairs
beckoning and beckoning
as I held away as long as I could bear
then I leaped upon the thing
sucking and tongueing,
hairs in my soul
cunt in my soul
you in my soul
in a miracle bed
with children screaming outside
while riding on skates
bicycles at
5 P.M. in the afternoon
at that wonderful hour of
5 P.M. in the afternoon
all the love poems were written:
my tongue entered your cunt and your soul
and the blue bedspread was there
and the children in the alley
and it sang and it sang and it sang and
it sang.

poem for Dante

Dante, baby, the Inferno
is here now.
I wish you could see
it. for some time
we've had the power to
blow up the earth
and now we're finding
the power to leave
it. but most will have to
stay and
die. either by the Bomb
or the refuse of stacked-up
bones
and other emptied containers,
and shit and glass and smoke,
Dante, baby, the Inferno
is here now.
and people still look at roses
ride bicycles
punch time clocks
buy homes and paintings and cars;
people continue to
copulate
everywhere, and the young look around

and scream
that this should be a better place,
as they've always done,
and then gotten old
and played the same dirty game.
only now
all the dirty games of the centuries
have added to a score that seems almost
impossible to right.
some still try—
we call them saints, poets, madmen, fools.
Dante, baby, o Dante, baby,
you should see us
now.

the conditions

presently, under the conditions of the sun
my world is ending.
marked by the worm,
haggled by a world population
that has no reference to me.
presently, under the conditions of the sun
my world is ending.
my friends, it has hardly ever been
a kind time.
I've shown courage, drunkenness and
fear.
the heart continues to work
through unquestionable terror.

under the conditions of the sun
I make ready to lay down
the labor, the pain and whatever
honor is left.

29 chilled grapes

the process of learning is devious

all these windmills

all this bloody transition

plugged sinks

toilet-paper minds

love's lie, that naked whore

dogs with more souls than Pittsburgh millionaires

wrecked men who thought grace more eternal than cunning

the process of living is too short and too long
too long for the old who never find out
too short for the old who found out
too soon for the young who never know
too much for the young who find out

the process of continuing is possible
with the aid of alcohol or dope or sex
or gold or golf or symphony music,
or deer hunting or learning to dance the funky chicken
or watching a baseball game or betting on a horse
or taking 6 hot baths a day
or hanging it onto yogi
or becoming a baptist or a guitar player
or getting a rubdown or reading the comics
or masturbating or eating 29 chilled grapes
or arguing about John Cage or going to the zoo
or smoking cigars or showing your pecker to little girls in the park
or being black and fucking a white girl
or being white and fucking a black girl
or walking a dog or feeding a cat or screaming at a child
or working a crossword puzzle or sitting in the park
or going to college or riding a bicycle or eating spaghetti
or going to poetry readings or giving poetry readings
or going to a movie or voting or traveling to India or
New York City or beating somebody up
or polishing silverware or shining your shoes
or writing a letter or waxing your car
or buying a new car or a throw rug
or a red shirt with white dots
or growing a beard or getting a crewcut
or standing on the corner sweating and looking wise
the process of continuing is possible.

the process of learning is devious

all those without hope
and never knowing it

the wildflower is the tiger who runs the universe
the tiger is the wildflower that runs the universe
and those mad and incomparable human creatures with roach souls
that I am beckoned to love and hate and live among,
these must truly someday vanish
in the dinosaur strength of their ugliness
so the sun will not feel so bad
so the sea can throw off the ships and oil and shit
so the sky can clear of their mean greed
so night can be told from day
so that treachery can become the palest of anachronisms
so that love, which probably began it all, can begin again
and last and last and last and last and last and last and
last and last and last and last

burning in water, drowning in flame

carbon copy people
choosing clothes and shoes and objects
carbon copy people
walking in and out of buildings,
seeing the same sun
the same moon,
reading the same paper
looking at the same programs
having the same ideas,
sleeping at the same time,
arising at the same time,
eating the same food,
driving the same cars down the same freeways
carbon copy people
with carbon copy children
in carbon copy houses
with carbon copy Christmases and New Years
and birthdays and lives and
deaths
and lawns and dishwashers and rugs
and vases and loves and copulations, and
they have carbon copy dentists and
carbon copy mayors and governors and presidents
all seeing the same sun and the same moon,

o carbon copy coffins
o carbon copy graves
o carbon copy funerals
under the same moon,
the carbon copy grass the frost
the carbon copy tombstones,
the carbon copy laughter
the carbon copy screams
the carbon copy jokes
the carbon copy poems
the carbon copy carbon copy
madmen and drunks and dope fiends and rapists
and cats and dogs and birds and snakes and spiders,
there is too much of everything all alike,
I have fingers and there are fingers everywhere,
if I enter a door I must exit a door,
I have shit and there is shit everywhere,
I have eyes and there are eyes everywhere,
I have nightmares and there are nightmares everywhere,
if I sleep I must awake,
if I fuck I must stop fucking,
if I eat I must stop eating,
I can't do anything I want to,
I am locked into a repetition of sameness . . .
I am burning in water
I am drowning in flame
I am released into sugar clouds that piss vinegar,
but so are you and so are they and so are we,
ant thoughts and ant struggles
against a dynamo of alikened contortions,
help help help help help help help
I scream the carbon copy help against the carbon copy sky,

that all this carbon and cardboard contains blood and pain,
even love and history and hope,
that's the hitch, or is it a trick?
how can we know? the carbon copy psychiatrists and preachers
and philosophers tell us carbon copy things . . .
death? is there death? perhaps the gate swings open
and we are welcomed by roasted and tortured angels
where we are finally gypped into an insufficient Eternity,
a gag worse than Life . . .
wouldn't that be shit?
to get away from men like gearshifts and women like
horsemeat, only to
unfold into worse? o,
think then of the angered suicides
the dead heroes of dead wars . . .
the run-over children,
the saints burnt at stake—
all of them short-changed, rolled, doped,
sold into a slavery worse than snot
sing your deaths sing your deaths sing your
deaths, sing your life, sing
life, this isn't any
good, this isn't any
good. good god, I forgot to put a
carbon under this
paper . . .

a cop-out to a possible immortality:

if we can't make literature out of our
agony

what are we going to do with
it?

beg in the streets?

I like my minor comforts
just like any other
son of a
bitch.

well, now that Ezra has died . . .

well, now that Ezra has died
we are going to have a great many poems written
about Ezra and what he meant and who he
was and how it went
and how it still is with
Ezra gone.
well, I was shacked with this alcoholic woman
for 7 years
and I kept packing home the *Cantos* through the
door, and she kept saying,
"For God's sake, you got POUND again? You know
you can't read him. Did you bring any
wine?"
she was right. I couldn't read the *Cantos*.
but I usually brought the wine
and we drank the
wine.
I don't know how many years I packed those
Cantos back and forth from the downtown public
library
but they were always available in the shelves of
the Literature and Philology section.

well, he died, and I finally went from wine to
beer; I suppose he was a great writer
it's just that I'm so lazy in my reading habits.
I detest any sort of immaculate strain,
but I still feel rather warm for him and Ernie
and Gertie and James J., all that gang
gripping to world war one
making the 20's and 30's available
in their special way; then there was world war 2,
Ezra backed a loser and got 13 years in with the
loonies, and now he's dead at 87 and his mistress is
alone.

well, this is just another Ezra Pound poem
except to say
I could never read or understand the *Cantos*
but I'll bet I carried them around more than
almost anybody, and all the young boys
are trying to check them out at the library
tonight.

warts

I remember my grandmother best
because of all her warts
she was 80 and the warts were
very large
I couldn't help staring at her
warts
she came to Los Angeles every Sunday
by bus and streetcar from Pasadena
her conversation was always the same
"I am going to bury all of you"
"you're not going to bury me,"
my father would say
"you're not going to bury me,"
my mother would say
then we'd sit down to a Sunday
dinner
after she left my mother would say,
"I think it's terrible the way she talks
about burying everybody."
but I rather liked it
her sitting there
covered with warts
and threatening to bury us
all

and when she ate her dinner
I'd watch the food going into her mouth
and I'd look at her
warts
I'd imagine her going to the bathroom
and wiping her behind
and thinking,
I am going to bury everybody
the fact that she didn't
was even rather sad to
me
one Sunday she simply wasn't
there, and it was a
much duller Sunday
somebody else was going to have to
bury us
the food hardly tasted
as well

my new parents

(for Mr. and Mrs. P. C.)

he's 60. she's 55. I'm 53.
we sit and drink in their
kitchen. we drink out of quart beerbottles
and chain-smoke.
we're dumb drunks. the hours go by.
we argue about religion, football,
movie stars.
I tell them I could be a movie star.
he tells me that he is a movie star.
a red radio plays in back
of us.
"you're my new parents," I tell them.
I get up and kiss each of them
on top of the head.
he's 60. she's 55. I'm 53.
my new parents.
I lift my quart of beer:
"I'll buy next time, I'll get the booze
next time."
they don't answer.
"I'll be back in the middle of January,
I'll bring a present, I'll bring a present

worth about 14 dollars."
"how's your teeth?" he asks.
"o.k., what's left of them."
"you need teeth you go to the U.S.C.
Medical School."
he reaches into his mouth
takes out one plate, then the
other. he lays them on the
table. "look at those teeth, can't get
better teeth than those. U.S.C. Medical
School."
"can you eat anything?" I ask.
"anything that moves," he says.
soon he is asleep
his head in his arms. she walks me to the
door.
I kiss my mother goodbye.
"you make me hot, you son of a bitch," she
says.
"now, mama," I say, "don't talk like that.
the good Lord is listening."
she closes the door and I walk down the
driveway
drunk in the moonlight.

something about the action:

that
     New York City traincrash was
something
        so near Christmas, no,
Thanksgiving
        bodies stacked with catsup &
not speaking—

        then the bolo knife
in the Philippines
        into the president's
wife on stage
       tv cameras on
she fell backwards
       he slashed;
3 broken fingers and 75 stitches later
she will recover
       a former beauty queen
she won't be
       quite so beautiful
now & then
3 guards shot the dirty son of a
bitch with the
bolo—

this guy's wife said she was
going to leave him for
good
so he said
            "let me come over and
we'll talk it over," and
he came over and they
talked it over and
she said
            "no," and
he took out a gun and shot her
head halfway off
                        then
killed the boy
                        age 2
the girl
            age 4
                        killed
his wife's sister
when she ran in through the
                                    door (she'd
been sprinkling the flowers
                        outdoors)
and then he
            walked outside and shot the first
guy he saw on the street
                        then
took the gun and shot his
                        own
head halfway
            off—

one guy
        he raised a man from the
dead
       right out of the grave
                   now
that's pretty good and he also
walked across WATER (not the guy
raised from the dead but the
other guy) &
          he also healed
lepers &
       made blind men
              see, and
he said
       Love one another and
Believe,
       then they nailed him
to the wood with big
            spikes &
he left and never came
           back—.

one of the wisest
          men, o, he was
pretty wise
       you can still read him
now
   he still reads
         good and wise
but some of the boys
          in government became

upset
        claimed mainly he was corrupting the
youth
and they
        locked him
                up &
offered him a cup of
                hemlock which
he accepted.
                I don't know if he
made his point
                he never
came back
        either
                but he's
in the library, anyhow, every-
body's got to leave, they
say—

        then
there was this
                looker
                        she
bandaged the
                soldiers and
sang little songs to
                them and
maybe kissed them behind the
                        ears
I'm not sure what went wrong
                        there, some

disagreement, they
                    stacked the wood
under her
          got it going
                  burned her
alive, Joan of Arc, what a
whore—

       then
there was this
            painter
                  he
painted like a child but
he was a
          man
and they say
            he painted pretty good
but he hardly knew how
to mix
          paints
            but he knew how to
paint the sun he made it
whirl on the canvas, and
                  the flowers
they whirled
            and his people sat over
tables
      his people sat very strangely
over tables and in
            chairs, and
his contemporaries
              mocked him

and children
                threw stones and broke his
windows,
                and what most people remember
about him was he
                        cut off his
ear and gave it to a
                        whore, not
Joan of Arc,
                I don't know her
name, and
                he went out in the fields and
sat in his whirling
                        sun and
killed himself.
                        now you may be able to
buy a Cadillac
                but I doubt if you will be able to
buy
    any of the paintings he
                                left
behind, he was pretty
good
    they say—

after 2 and one half
                        years of
marriage
            then divorce
                        my x-
wife wrote me every
                        Christmas for

8 years,
        quite long bits:
but mainly:
            she said:
I have 2 children
                now
                    my husband
Yena is very
            sensitive,
I have written one book on
                            incest
another on child behavior patterns
still looking for a
                publisher
Yena has moved to San
                    Francisco I may
go back to Texas
                mother died
2 books of my children's stories have been
accepted
            the oldest boy looks very much like
Yena
    I am still painting
                    you always liked my
paintings but painting takes so much
out of me
            I am still teaching public school
I like it
        we had a storm up here this
winter
        locked in
                absolutely for 2

weeks
     no out in up or down
               sitting still and
waiting
     barbara

         after 8 years she stopped
writing
     Christmas returned to
             normal and
I got the wax
     cleaned out of my
ears.

55 beds in the same direction

these brilliant midnights
gabardine snakes passing through
walls, sounds
broken by car crashes of drunks in
ten-year-old cars

you know it's soiled again and then
again

it's in these brilliant midnights
while fighting moths and tiny
mosquitoes,
your woman behind you
twisting in the blankets
thinking you no longer love her;
that's untrue, of course,
but the walls are familiar and
I've liked walls
I've praised walls:
give me a wall and I'll give you a way—
that's all I asked in
exchange. but I suppose I meant:
I'll give you my
way.

it's very difficult to compose a
sonnet while sleeping in a flophouse with
55 snoring men
in 55 beds all pointed in the same direction.

I'll tell you what I thought:
these men have lost both chance and
imagination.

you can tell as much about men in the
way they snore as in the way they
walk, but then
I was never much at sonnets.

but once I thought I'd find all great men on
skid row,
I once thought I'd find great men down there
strong men who had discarded society,
instead I found men who society had fiddled
away.

they were dull
inept and
still
ambitious.

I found the bosses more
interesting and more alive than the
slaves.

and that was hardly romantic. one would like things
romantic.

55 beds pointed in the same
direction and
I couldn't sleep
my back hurt
and there was a steady feeling on my
forehead like a piece of
sheet metal.

it really wasn't very terrible but somehow
it was very impossible.

and I thought,
all these bodies and all these toes and all
these fingernails and all these hairs in
assholes and all this stink

immaculate and accepted mauling of
things,
can't we do something with it?

no chance, came the answer, they don't
want it.

then, looking all about
all those 55 beds pointed in the same
direction
I thought,
all these men were babies once
all these men were cuddly and
pink (except the black ones and the yellow ones
and the red ones and the others).

they cried and they felt,
had a way.

now they've become
sophisticated
phlegmatic
unwanteds.

I got
out.

I got between 4 walls
alone.

I gave myself a brilliant
midnight. other brilliant midnights
arrived. it wasn't that
difficult.

but if they had been there:
(those men) I would have stayed there with
them.

if I can save you the same years of error
let me:

the secret is in the walls
listening to a small radio
rolling cigarettes
drinking
        coffee
        beer

water
grape juice
a lamp burning near you
it comes along—
the names
the history
a flow a flow
the downward glance of psyche
the humming effect
the burning of monkeys.

the brilliant midnight walls:
there's no stopping even as your head rolls
under the bed and the cat buries
its excreta.

b

――――――――――――――――

the wisdom of the
bumblebee crawling
the handle of the
water pitcher is
enormous as the
sun comes through
the kitchen win-
dow I think again
of the murder of
Caesar and down in
the sink are three
dirty water glasses.

the doorbell rings
and I stand deter-
mined not to answ-
er.

finger

you had your finger in her pussy,
she said.
no, I said, it's just touching
the outside.
well, it looks like you had your
finger in her pussy, she
said.
no, I said, it's on the outside.

suddenly she tore the photo
up.

o for christ's sake,
Annie, what did you do that for?
said everybody in the
room.

Annie ran into my bathroom and
slammed the door.
somebody rolled a joint and we
passed it
around.

the thing

far away into the bluebird night
is that mighty thing that might save us;
down under the bridge it sits
poking matches under its fingernails,
then lighting them;
it has lips like my father
eyes like a frightened monkey
and on its back
5 air mail stamps are stuck
randomly;
this thing knows but it won't talk,
it can run but it prefers to sit,
it can sing but it would rather grunt;
it intimidates ants, breathes beetles
into its nose;
it weeps, it laughs, it farts;
sometimes at night it will
approach your bed and yank a
hair from one of your ears;
it delights in essential dullness,
can't tie knots;
it remembers odd things like
curled and dried banana skins
fallen from trash cans;

it's shy out of cowardliness
and brave only in short flashes;
it can't drive a car
or
swim
multiply
add or
divide;
it smells its toes
it dreams of popcorn and glass toads;
it could save us but it won't;
it doesn't want us;
someday it will invade the sun;
but now we sit in our rooms and wait,
we stop at signals and wait,
we have sex and wait,
we don't have sex and wait.
it laughs when we weep,
it weeps when we laugh;
it waits with us.

Bob Dylan

these two young ones
in the court across from me
they play Bob Dylan
all day and all night
on their stereo

they turn that stereo
as high as it can go
and it's a very good
stereo

the whole neighborhood
gets Bob Dylan
free

and I get him freest of all
because I live in the court
across the way

I get Dylan when I shit
I get Dylan when I fuck
and just before I try to
sleep.

sometimes I see them
outside on the sidewalk
quite young and neat
going out for food and
toilet paper

they are one of the loveliest
couples in the
neighborhood.

"Texsun"

she's from Texas and weighs
103 pounds
and she stands before the
mirror combing strands and
strands of reddish hair
which falls all the way down
her back to her ass.
the hair is magic and shoots
sparks and I lay on the bed
and watch her combing her
hair. she's like a nymph
out of the movies but she's
actually there. we make love
at least once a day and
she can make me laugh
with any sentence she cares
to say. Texas women have always
been immensely beautiful and
healthy, and besides that she's
cleaned my refrigerator, my sink,
the bathroom, and she cooks and
feeds me healthy foods
and washes the dishes to top
that.

"Hank," she told me,
holding up a can of grapefruit
juice, "this is the best of them
all."
it says "Texsun—unsweetened
PINK grapefruit juice."

she looks like Katharine Hepburn
must have looked while she was
in high-school, and I watch those
103 pounds
combing a yard and some change
of glinting reddish hair
before the mirror
and I can feel her inside of my
wrists and at the backs of my eyes,
and the toes and legs and belly
of me feel her and
the other part too,
and all of Los Angeles falls down
and weeps in joy,
the walls of the love parlors shake,
the ocean rushes in and she turns
to me and says, "damn this hair!"
and I say,
"yes."

warm water bubbles

what I like
is when I'm in the bathtub
and I fart
and that fart is so bad
that I can smell the stink
of it
up through the water.

the pleasure of power:
Mahatma Gandhi dying.
the iris in drag.

love is wonderful
but so is the stench of the
innards,
the coming forth of the hidden
parts.
the fart. the turd. the death of
a lung.

bathtub rings, shit-rings in toilets
dying bulls dragged across Mexican dirt
Benito Mussolini and his whore Claretta
being hung by their heels

and torn to pieces by the mob—
these things have more gentle glory
than any Christ with His
perfectly-placed wounds.

I read (and I no longer know which side
did it) that in the Russian revolution
they'd catch a man, cut him open, nail
part of his intestine to a tree
then force him to run around and around
that tree, rolling his intestines about
the trunk. I'm no sadist. I'd probably
weep if I had to see it, probably go mad.
but I do know that we are much more than
we think we are
even though the romantics
concentrate upon the hate/and or/love of
the heart.

a fart in the bathtub contains a whole
essential history of the human race.
love is so wonderful.
so is the fart.
especially mine.
dying bulls being dragged across the Mexican
dirt and me in the bathtub
looking up at a 60-watt bulb and feeling all right.

a corny poem

we lived in a hotel next to a
vacant lot
where somebody was growing a
garden
which included these long
cornstalks
and we came out of the corner bar
at 2 A.M.
and started walking
toward our place
and when we got to the vacant
lot she said, "I want some
corn!"
and I followed her out and
I said, "shit, this stuff
isn't ripe yet . . ."
"yes, it is . . . I've got to
have some corn . . ."
we were always hungry and
she started ripping off
these ears of corn and
stuffing them into her purse
and down her blouse and
I looked up the street and

saw the squad car coming
and I said, "it's the cops,
run!"
they had the red lights on
and we ran toward our
apartment house, down the
front walk . . .
"HALT OR I'LL FIRE!"
and down the stairway to
the basement elevator
which happened to be there
and we closed the doors and
hit the button #4
as they stood down there
pushing buttons. we got
out and left the elevator
doors open, ran down to our
apartment, got in, locked the door
and sat in the dark
listening and drinking cheap
wine. we heard them out there
walking around. they finally
gave up but we left the lights
out and she boiled the ears of
corn, we sat in the dark a
long time listening to the ears
of corn boil and drinking the
cheap wine. we took the corn
out and tried to eat it. it
was undeveloped, we were nibbling
at murders, at miscarriages of
nature.

"I told you this shit wasn't ready,"
I said.
"it's ready," she said, "for Christ's
sake, eat it!"
"I've tried," I said, "Lord God knows
how I've tried . . ."
"be glad you've got this corn," she said,
"be glad you've got me."
"the corn is green," I said, "green as
caterpillars in April . . ."
"it's good, it's good, this corn is *good*,"
she said
and started throwing ears of it at me.
I threw the ears back.
we finished the wine and went to sleep.
in the morning when we awakened here were
these tiny little ears of corn all over the
rug and on the sofa and on the chairs.
"where'd this crap come from?" she asked.
"the Jolly Green Giant," I said, "shit us
a tubful."
"in this world," she said, "a girl can
never tell what she's going to wake up
with."
"something hard," I answered, "is better
than nothing."
she got up and took a shower and I turned
over and went back to sleep.

the ladies of the afternoon

no more ladies knock on my door
at 3 A.M.
with ready bottle and ready body;
they arrive at 2:30 in the afternoon
and talk about the soul,
and they look better than the old girls
did, but the understanding is clear—
no one-night stands,
I must buy the whole package;
they know Manet from Mozart, they know all the
Millers, and will sip on a bit of wine
but just a bit, and their breasts are vast and
firm
and their asses are sculptured by
sex-fiends;
they know the philosophers, the politicians and
the tricks;
they have minds *and* bodies,
and they sit and look at me and say,
"you seem a little nervous. is everything
all right?"
"o yes," I say, "fine," thinking what the hell is
this?

I'm not going to waste a month to get a pinch of
buttock;
and such terribly beautiful eyes, o yes,
the witches!
how they smile, knowing what you are
thinking—
to place them on a bed and be done with it—
fuck yes!—
but this is an inflationary age
and with them
you must pay first, during and
afterwards. it's
the emancipated female, and I am no longer a
schoolboy, and I allow them to leave
untouched, most of them with a wrecked man or two
behind them already,
and still in their 20's, and a meeting is arranged for later
in the week, and they leave
dangling their eternal price
behind them
like their beautiful asses,
but I find myself writing,
the next day,
"Dear K . . . : Your beauty and youth are simply too
much for me. I do not deserve
you, so therefore I ask that we break our relationship,
as small as that may have
been . . .
      yours,
        . . ."

then I smile, fold the letter, put it in the envelope, lick it
closed, add stamp,
and I walk down the street
to the nearest mailbox
keeping the emancipated woman as free as she
should be, and not doing too badly
toward myself
either.

tongue-cut

he lives in the back and comes to my door
carrying his shotgun in one hand.
"listen," he says, "there was a guy sitting
on your couch on the porch while you were
gone. he didn't act right. I asked him what
he wanted, he said he wanted to see you.
I told him you weren't in. do you know a
tall black guy named 'Dave'?"
"I dunno nobody like that . . ."
"I saw this guy on the street later and I
asked him what he was doing in the neighbor-
hood."
"I don't know no tall black named 'Dave.'"
"I've been watching your place. I ran off a couple
of those Germans. you don't want to see any Germans,
do you?"
"no, Max, I don't like Germans, Frenchmen and especially
I don't like Englishmen. Mexicans and Greeks are all
right but there is something I don't like about the looks on their
faces."
"there have been more Germans than any other kind."
"run them off . . ."
"o.k., I will . . . when you leaving town again?"
"tomorrow."

"tomorrow . . . ?"
"tomorrow, yes, and if you find some fucker sitting on
my porch couch, blow his god damned head off . . ."
"o.k., I will . . ."
"thanks, Max . . ."
"it's all right . . ."
he walks back to his court in the back with his
shotgun and
goes inside.

"my god," says Linda Lee, "you know what you've
done?"
"yes," I say.
"he believes in you. when we come back there'll be
a dead body on the porch."
"all right . . ."
"don't you remember when I took my day of silence?
you told him you had cut my tongue out . . . and he
accepted it matter of factly . . ."
"Max is the only real buddy I've
got . . ."
"you're an accessory to the fact . . ."
"I don't like uninvited guys sitting around on my porch
couch waiting for me . . ."
"suppose it's some poet, some guy who admires your
work?"
"like I said, 'Max is the only real buddy I've got.'
let's start packing . . ."
"what happened to my green dress?"
she asks.

Venice, Calif., nov. 1977:

leary's long gone and the drop-out area he created:
the junkies, the crazies, the fanatics, the general
rush of idiots have long ago been taken care of by
the institutions, including the institution of death.
lsd is almost out, speed is standard, reds are rare,
joints aren't brave, coke and H are too expensive,
roller-skates and racquet-ball are in; less guitars,
less bongos, less blacks; the natives now huckster baggage
and small items from vans while their stereo sets
no longer play Bob Dylan, they have become minor
capitalists, nothing wearying, just a hype, and the
ten-speed bike, they ride the ten-speed bike as if
in the dream, all the revolutions are over but there is
still an anarchist or two under the palms, tamping their
pipes and planning to blow up some damn thing for no
damned reason and the sea goes in and out, out and in,
and over in Santa Monica the musclemen are still there,
although they aren't the same musclemen, and the sea
goes in and out, and there's no Vietnam to protest, hardly
anything to do, racquet-ball, roller-skates and ten-speed,
and fucking is almost a bore, it means trouble, you know,
and cheap wine is in, and you can use a do-it-yourself car
wash for twenty-five cents.

mirror

women at my dresser mirror
there have been so many women
at my dresser mirror
combing their hair
the comb catching
and I see in their eyes in
the mirror as they look
at me
stretched on the bed.
I am almost always on the bed
it's my favorite place.

that love or even
relationships
stop
seems so very odd
but that new loves
new relationships
arrive
that's lucky.

even though solitude is
good
loneliness seems
imperfect.

all those faces in the
mirror
I remember them.
blossoms of feeling and
humor,
I've been treated well
most of the
time.

the women are now
in front of other mirrors
and the men stretch on the beds
I'm sure—
conversing, or
silent, relaxing.

another woman uses
my mirror
her name is Linda Lee
she laughs at me
I have on a black and white
Japanese "happy coat."

maybe she will stay in my
mirror.

head jobs

she's still doing it.
she sculpts men's heads
then goes to bed with
them
I guess to match the clay
with the flesh.

that's how I met
her.

I didn't object
but in such cases
you always feel that it is
you.

but afterwards
I found out
that I was not the
first

and after I began living with
her
I'd look at these sculpted heads
of men
on this table
and on top of the tv set
and
here and there
and I'd think,
my oh my.

and then she'd tell me,
"listen, you know whose head I'd
like to sculpt?"

"uh uh."

"I'd like to sculpt big Mike
Swinnert . . . he has an interesting skull . . .
did you ever notice his mouth, his
teeth?"

"yes, I have . . ."

"I like his wife too. but I think I'd like
to do Mike first . . . you wouldn't be
jealous, would you?"

"ah, no. I'll go to the track or something
so you can concentrate . . ."

"it's kind of embarrassing for me to
ask him. he's your friend. would you
mind asking . . . ?"

Mike didn't have a car so I picked him
up and drove him over. as I parked outside
he said, "listen, I can fuck her if I want
to, you know. do you mind if I fuck her?"
"well, I guess I would," I said.
he gave me that glance: "all right,
for your sake, I won't."

I walked him into the clay and then went
back downstairs.

I drove out to the track and had
a terrible day at the
track . . .

I once walked through McArthur Park
with her as she picked out men with
interesting heads and
I went up to them and asked if she
might sculpt their heads. I even
offered them money. they all
refused, feeling that something was
wrong. I too felt that something was
wrong, especially with me.

it wasn't much after that when
the sculptress and I
split.

she even moved out of town but
I found myself flying to this other
state to see her—twice. and
each time noticing
more men's heads about her
apartment.

"who's this guy?" I asked her
about one of them.

"oh, that's Billyboy, the bronco
rider . . ."

I left 2 or 3 days
later . . .

lives continued and 2 or 3 women later
my friend Jack Bahiah came by. we
talked of this and that, then Jack
mentioned that he had flown out to
see the sculptress.

"did she do your head, Jack?"

"yeah, man, she did my head but it
didn't look like me, man. guess who
it looked like, man?"

"I dunno, man . . ."

"it looked like you . . ."

"Jack, my man, you always had a great line
of shit . . ."

"no shit, man, no shit . . ."

Jack and I drank much wine that night, he's
pretty good at pouring it down.

"I was holding her in my arms in the bed
and she said, 'God, I love him, Jack, I
miss him!' and then she started crying."

I didn't hate him at all for fucking her
for sleeping against her when I had slept
against her for 5 or 6 years, and that shows
the durability of humans: we can roust it
out and punch it down and forget it.

I know that she's still sculpting men's
heads and can't stop. she once told me
that Rodin did something similar in a
slightly different way. all right.

I wish her the luck of the clay and
the luck of the men. it's been a long
night into noon, sometimes, for most
of us.

chili and beans

hang them upside down through the plentiful
night,
burn their children and molest their crops,
cut the throats of their wives,
shoot their dogs, pigs and servants;
whatever you don't kill, enslave;
your politicians will make you heroes,
courts of international law will rule
your victims guilty;
you will be honored, given medals,
pensions, villas along the river
with your choice of pre-prostitute
women;
the priests will open the doors of God
to you.

the important thing is victory,
it always has been;
you will be ennobled,
you will be promoted as the humble and
gracious conqueror
and you will believe it.

what it means is that the human mind
is not yet ready
so you will claim a victory for the
human spirit.

a cut throat can't answer.
a dead dog can't bite.

you've won.
proclaim the decency.

go to your grave cleanly—

nobody cares
nobody really cares
didn't you know?
didn't you remember?
nobody really cares

even those footsteps
walking toward somewhere
are going nowhere

you may care
but nobody cares—
that's the first step
toward wisdom

learn it

and nobody has to care
nobody is supposed to care

sexuality and love are flushed away
like shit

nobody cares

learn it

belief in the impossible is the
trap
faith kills

nobody cares—
the suicides, the dead, the gods
or the living

think of green, think of trees, think
of water, think of luck and glory of a
sort
but cut yourself short
quickly and finally
of depending upon the love
or expecting the love of
another

nobody cares.

kuv stuff mox out

gunned down outside the Seaside Motel I stand looki
ng at the live lobster in a fishshop on the Redondo
Beach pier the redhead gone to torture other males
it's raining again it's raining again and again som
etimes I think of Bogart and I don't like Bogart an
y more kuv stuff mox out—when you get a little mon
ey in the bank you can write down anything on the p
age call it Art and pull the chain gunned down in a
fish market the lobsters you see they get caught lik
e we get caught. think of Gertie S. sitting there
telling the boys how to get it up. she was an ocea
n liner I prefer trains pulling boxcars full of gun
s underwear pretzels photos of Mao Tse-tung barbell
s kuv stuff mox out—(write mother) when you flower
my stone notice the fly on your sleeve and think of
a violin hanging in a hockshop. many hockshops hav
e I been gunned down in best one in L.A. they pull
a little curtain around he who wishes to hock and h
e who *might* pay something. it's an Art hockshops a
re needed like F. Scott Fitz was needed which makes
us pause this moment: I like to watch live lobster
s they are fire under water hemorrhoids—gross othe
r magic—balls!: they are lobsters but I like to w
atch them when I if I should get rich I will get a

KUV STUFF MOX OUT

gunned down outside the Seaside
Motel
I stand looking at live lobster
in a fishshop on the Redondo Beach
pier
the redhead gone to torture
other males
it's raining again
it's raining again and again
sometimes I think of Bogart and
I don't like Bogart any more
kuv stuff mox out--
when you get a little money in
the bank
you can write anything down
on the page you want
to
call it Art and pull the
chain
gunned down in a fishmarket
the lobsters you see
they get caught like we
get caught.
think of Gertie S.
sitting there telling the boys
how to get it
up.
she was like an ocean liner
I prefer trains pulling boxcars full

First page of the first 10-page draft.

large glass tank say ten feet by four by four and I
'll sit and watch them for hours while drinking the
white moselle I am drinking now and when people com
e by I will chase them away like I do now. I mean,
some people say change means growth well certain per
manent acts also prevent decay like flossing fuckin
g fencing fatting belching and bleeding under a hun
dred watt General Electric bulb. novels are nice m
ice are fussy and my lawyer tells me that Abraham L
incoln did some shit that never got into the histor
y books—which makes it the same wall up and down.
never apologize. understand the sorrow of error. b
ut never. don't apologize to an egg a serpent a lo
ver. gunned down in a green taxi outside Santa Cru
z with an AE-I in my lap grifted in the pickpocket'
s hand slung like a ham. was it Ginsberg did a may
pole dance in Yugoslavia to celebrate May D
ay catch me doing that and you can cut both my back
pockets off. you know I never heard my mother piss
. I've heard many women piss but now that I think
of it I can't ever remember hearing my mother piss.
I am not particular about planets I don't dislike t
hem I mean like peanut shells in an ashtray that's
planets. sometimes every 3 or 4 years you see a fa
ce it is usually not the face of a child but that f
ace makes an astonishing day even though the light
is in a certain way or you were driving by in an a
utomobile or you were walking and the face was movi
ng past in a bus or an auto it make that day of the
moment like a brain-jolt something to tell you it's
always solitary being gunned down while slipping a
stick of gum out of the wrapper outside Hollywood's

oldest pool parlor on the west side of Western belo
w the boulevard. the gross is net and the net is g
ross and Gertie S. never showed her knees to the bo
ys and Van Gogh was a lobster a roasted peanut. I
think that "veer" is a splendid word and it's still
raining gunned down in water waterbags worth of pig
's snouts cleverly like cigarettes for men and for
women I care enough to proclaim liberty throughout
the land then wonder why nuns are nuns butchers tha
t and fat men remind me of glorious things breathin
g dust through their hems. if I gunned down Bogar
t he'd spit out his cigarette grab his left side in
black and white striped shirt look at me through a
butterfat eye and drop. if meaning is what we do w
e do plenty if meaning isn't what we do check squar
e #9 it probably falls halfway in between which sus
tains balance and the poverty of the poor and fire
hydrants mistletoe big dogs on big lawns behind iron
fences. Gertie S., of course, was more interested
in the word than the feeling and that's clearly fai
r because men of feeling (or women) (or) (you see)
(how nice) (I am) usually become creatures of Actio
n who fail (in a sense) and are recorded by the peo
ple of words whose works usually fail not matter. (
how nice). roll and roll and roll it keeps raining
gunned down in a fish market by an Italian with bad
breath who never knew I fed my cat twice a day and
never masturbated while he was in the same room. no
w you know in this year of 1978 I paid $8441.32 to
the government and $2419.84 to the State of Califor
nia because I sat down to this typewriter usually d
runk after the horse races and I don't even use a ma

jor commercial publisher and I used to live off of
one nickel candy bar a day typewriter in hock I pri
nted my stuff with a pen and it came back. I mean,
fellow dog, men sometimes turn into movies. and som
etimes movies can get to be not so good. pray for
me. I don't apologize. cleverness is not the out
endurance helps if you can hit the outside spiker
at 5:32 twilight—bang! the Waner brothers used to
bat two three for the Pirates now only 182 people i
n Pittsburgh remember them and that's exactly proper
. what I didn't like about that Paris gang was tha
t they made too much of writing but nobody can say
that they didn't get it down as well as possible wh
en all the heads and eyes seemed to be looking else
where that's why in spite of all the romanticism at
tached I go along not for the propaganda but for th
e sillier reasons of luck and the way. my lobsters
horses and lobsters and white moselle and there's a
good woman near me after all of the bad or the seem
ing bad. Rachmaninoff is on now on the radio and I
finish my second bottle of moselle. what a lovely
emotional hound he was my giant black cat stretched
across the rug the rent is paid the rain has stoppe
d there is a stink to my fingers my back hurts gunn
ed down I fall roll those lobsters examine them the
re's a secret there they hold pyramids drop them al
l the women of the past all the avenues doorknobs bu
ttons falling from shirt I never heard my mother pi
ss and I never met your father I think that we'd ha
ve drunk enough, properly.

a long hot day at the track

out at the track all day burning in the sun
they turned it all upside down, sent in all
the longshots. I only had one winner, a 6
to one shot. it's on days like that you notice
the hoax is on.

I was in the clubhouse. I usually meet the
maître d' of *Musso's* in the clubhouse. that
day I met my doctor. "where the hell you been?"
he asked me. "nothing but hangovers lately,"
I told him. "you come by anyhow. you don't
have to be sick. we'll have lunch. I know a
Thai place, we'll eat Thai food. you still
writing that porno stuff?" "yeah," I said,
"it's the only way I can make it." "let me
sit with you," he said, "I've got the 6."
"I've got the 6 too," I said, "that means
we're fucked."

we sat down and he told me about his four
wives: the first one didn't want to copulate.
the second wanted to go skiing at
Aspen all the time. the third one was
crazy. the fourth one was all right, they'd
been together seven years.

the horses came out of the gate. the doctor
just looked at me and talked about his fourth
wife. he was some talking doctor. I used to
get dizzy spells listening to him as I sat on
the edge of the examination table. but he had
brought my child into the world and he had sliced
out my hemorrhoids.

he went on about his fourth wife . . .

the race was 6 furlongs and unless it's a pack
of slow maidens 6 furlongs are usually run
somewhere between one minute and nine or ten
seconds. the one horse was 24 to one and had
jumped out to a three length lead. the son of
a bitch looked like he had no intention of
stopping.

"look," I said, "aren't you going to watch
the race?"

"no," he said, "I can't stand to watch, it
upsets me too much."

he began on his fourth wife again.

"hold it," I said, "they're coming down the
stretch!"

the 24 to one had 5 lengths at the wire. it
was over.

then after the first race my doctor sat down beside me.
he looked like he had just gotten out of surgery and
hadn't washed very well. he stayed until after the
8th race, talking, drinking beer and eating hot dogs.
then he started in about my liver: "you drink so god
damned much I want to take a look at your liver. you
come see me now." "all right," I said, "Tuesday after-
noon."

I remembered his receptionist. last time I had been there
the toilet had overflowed and she had got down on the floor
on her knees to wipe it up and her dress had pulled up
high above her thighs. I had stood there and watched,
telling her that Man's two greatest inventions had been
the atom bomb and plumbing.

then my doctor was gone and my biographer was gone too
and I was $97 ahead.
down at Del Mar they have that short stretch and they
come wailing off that last curve, and the water from the
fountains tastes like piss.

if my liver was gone it was gone; something always went
first and then the remainder followed. some parade.
it wasn't true, though, it depended upon the part.
I knew some people without minds who were blossoms of
health.

I lost the last race and drove on in lucky enough to
get some Shostakovich on the radio
and when you figure 6:20 P.M. on an AM radio
that's drawing a king to ace, queen, jack, ten . . .

"there's no logic to any of this stuff out here,"
said the doctor.

"I know," I said, "but the question I want you to
answer is: 'why are we out here?'"

he opened his wallet and showed me a photo of
his two children. I told him that they were very
nice children and that there was one race left.

"I'm broke," he said, "I've got to go. I've lost
$425."

"all right, goodbye." we shook hands.

"phone me," he said, "we'll eat at the Thai place."

the last race wasn't any better: they ran in a
9 to one shot who was stepping up in class and
hadn't won a race in two years.

I went down the escalator with the losers. it
was a hot Thursday in July. what was my doctor
doing at the racetrack on a Thursday? suppose
I'd had cancer or the clap? Jesus Christ, you
couldn't trust anybody anymore.

I'd read in the paper in between races
where these kids had busted into this
house and had beaten a 96-year-old woman
to death and had almost beaten to death
her 82-year-old blind sister or daughter,

I didn't remember. but they had taken a
color television set.

I thought, if they catch me out here
tomorrow I deserve to lose. I'm not
going to be here, I don't think I
will.

I walked toward my car with the next
day's *Racing Form* curled up in my
right hand.

the letters of John Steinbeck

I dreamt I was freezing and when I woke up and found
I wasn't freezing I somehow shit the bed.
I had been working on the travel book that night and
hadn't done much good and they were taking my horse
away, moving them to Del Mar.
I'd have time to be a writer now. I'd wake up in the
morning and there the machine would be looking at me
it would look like a tarantula; not so—it would look
like a black frog with fifty-one warts.

you figure Camus got it because he let somebody else
drive the car. I don't like anybody else driving the
car, I don't even like to drive it myself. well,
after I cleaned the shit off I put on my yellow
walking shorts and drove to the track. I parked and
went in.

the first one I saw was my biographer. I saw him
from the side and ducked. he was cleanly-dressed,
smoked a pipe and had a drink in his hand.
last time over at my place he gave me two books:
Scott and Ernest and *The Letters of John Steinbeck*.
I read those when I shit. I always read when I shit
and the worse the book the better the bowel movement

and the trivial lives of royalty never excited me either . . .

I never minded getting wet, often I would come into
places during a rain and somebody would say: "You're
WET!" as if I had no understanding of the circumstances.

but it seems that I am almost always in trouble with
most minds: "do you know that you haven't combed your
hair in the back?"

"your left shoe is untied . . ."

"I think your watch is five minutes slow . . ."

"your car needs a wash . . ."

when they drop that first bomb around here they'll
know why I've ignored everything to begin with.

the raindrops of myself finally gone wandering
nowhere
say like the Boston Strangler.
or like all the little girls with their little
curls
sitting and waiting.

letter to a friend with a domestic problem:

———————————————————

Hello Carl:
don't worry about your wife running away from you
she just didn't understand you.
I got a flat tire on the freeway today
and had to change the wheel with these coke-
heads breezing their Maseratis past my
ass.
the main thing is to just go about your business
and keep doing what you have to do, or better—
what you want to do.

I was in the dentist's office the other day
and I read this medical journal
and it said
all you got to do
is to live until the year 2020 A.D. and then
if you have enough money
when your body dies they can transplant your
brain into a fleshless body that gives you
eyesight and movement—like you can ride a
bicycle or anything like that and also you
don't have to bother with urinating or defe-
cating or eating—you just get this little

tank of blood in the top of your head filled
about once a month—it's kind of like oil
to the brain.
and don't worry, there's even sex, they say,
only it's a little different (haha) you can
ride her until she begs you to get off!
(she'll only leave you because of too much
instead of too little.)
that's the *fleshless* transplant bit.

but there's another alternative: they can
transplant your brain into a *living* body
whose brain has been removed so that there
will be space for yours.
only the cost for this will be more
prohibitive
as they will have to locate a body
a living body somewhere
say like in a madhouse or a prison or
off the street somewhere—maybe a kidnap—
and although these bodies will be better,
more realistic, they won't last as long as
the fleshless body which can go on about
500 years before need of replacement.
so it's all a matter of choice, what you
care for, or what you can afford.

when you get into the living body it isn't going
to last as long—they say about 110 years by
2020 A.D.—and then you're going to have to find
a living body replacement (again) or go for one
of the fleshless jobs.

generally, it is inferred in this article I read
in my dentist's office, if you're not so rich
you go for the fleshless job but
if you're still heavy into funds you
go for the living-body type all over again.
(the living-body types have some advantages
as you'll be able to fool most of the street
people and also
the sex life is more realistic although
shorter.)

Carl, I am not giving this thing exactly as
it was written but I am transferring all that
medical mumbo-jumbo down into something that we
can understand,
but do you think dentists ought to have crap like
this
lying around on their tables?
anyhow, probably by the time you get this letter
your old lady will be back with you.

anyhow, Carl, I kept reading on
and this guy went on to say that
in both the brain transplants into the
living body and into the fleshless body
something else would happen to these people who
had enough money to do these transfer tricks:
the computerized knowledge of the centuries would be
fed into the brain—and any way you wanted to go
you could go: you'd be able to paint like
Rembrandt or Picasso,
conquer like Caesar. you could do all the things

those and others like them had done
only better.
you'd be more brilliant than Einstein—
there would be very little that you could not do
and maybe the next body around you
could do that.

it gets rather dizzifying about there—
the guy goes on
he's kind of like those guys in their
Maseratis on coke; he goes on to say
in his rather technical and hidden language that
this is not Science Fiction
this is the opening of a door of horror and wonder
never wondered of before and he says that the
Last War of Man will be between the transplanted
computer-fed rich and of the non-rich who are
the Many
who will finally resent being screwed out of
immortality
and the rich will want to protect it
forever
and
that
in the end
the computer-fed rich will win the last
War of Man (and
Woman).

then he goes on to say that the next New
War will take shape as the
Immortal fights the Immortal

and what will follow will be an
exemplary
occurrence
so that Time as we know it
gives up.

now, that's some shit, isn't it,
Carl?
I would like to say
that in the light of all this
that your wife running away doesn't mean
much
but I know it does
I only thought I'd let you know
that other things could happen.

meanwhile, things aren't good here
either.
   your buddy,
    Hank

agnostic

read the other day
where a man wanted to exorcise the devil
out of his two children
so he tied them to a floor furnace and
roasted them to death.

I suppose that to believe in the devil
you have to believe in God
first.

I was taught to capitalize "God"
and some would say
that since I do that
is proof enough.

meanwhile, I use my Furnace to keep
warm
and I stay out of
Arguments.

clones

he told me, I had loaned this guy
200.
then he vanished.
I heard he went to Europe.
I figured not to worry about
it: the money was
gone.

no use losing your god damned
sleep, I said.

anyhow, he continued, I was in
the clubhouse the other night
at the harness meet.
I was in a betting line and I
saw this guy two lines
over.

and he looked like the guy you
loaned the 2 centuries to? I
asked.

right, he answered, Mike, he
looked like Mike.
only Mike was always well-
dressed and polished,
this guy was in old clothes,
he had a dirty beard and was
red-eyed like some
cheap wino.

I gotta cut down on my
drinking, I said.

anyhow, it so happened we
both finished our bets at
about the same time.
I walked off.

no use losing your sleep,
I said.

then, he continued, I felt
a pull at my elbow.
"Marty," he said and handed
me the 200.

a most stunning occurrence, I said.

yeah, said Marty, I thanked him
then went out to watch the
race.

sure, I said.

well, he continued, I won that
race.
and as the night went on I won
a few more.
it was a good night for
me.

when you're hot, I said, you're
hot.

anyhow, he went on, just before
the last race this guy came up
to me and he said, "hey, Marty,
I've hit the wall, lend me a
fifty."

yeah? I asked.

yeah, he said, now listen to
this good. first we had this
guy who looked like Mike only
he looked more like a cheap
wino, right?

right, I said.

o.k., he said, now this guy
looked like the guy who looked
like Mike only he didn't quite
look like the guy who looked like

Mike, it was more like he was
pretending to look like the guy
who looked like Mike.

everybody seems to get to look
alike after 8 or 9 races, I
said.

right, said Marty, so I told
him, "I don't know you."
I placed a 50 buck win bet on
the 4 horse, then
took the escalator down
to the parking lot.

no use losing your god damned
sleep, I said.

I didn't, he said, I went home,
drank a pint of Cutty Sark
and slept 'til noon.

gnawed by dull crisis

it's not easy
sending out these rockets to
nowhere.
I keep burning my fingers,
get spots of light before my
eyes.

the cats stare at me.

the calendar falls from the wall.

I need an easy midnight in the
Bahamas.
I need to watch
waterfalls of glory.
I need a maiden's fingers to
tie my shoes.
I need the dream
the sweet blue dream
the sweet green dream
the tall lavender dream.

I need the easy walk to Paradise.
I need to laugh the way I used to laugh.

I need to watch a good movie in a dark room.
I need to be a good movie in a dark room.

I want to borrow some of the natural courage
of the tiger.
I want to walk down alleys of China while
drunk.
I want to machinegun the swallow.
I want to drink wine with the assassins.
I wonder where Clark Gable's false teeth are
tonight?

I want John Fante to have legs and eyes again.
I know that the dogs will come to
tear the meat from the bones.
how can we sit about and watch baseball games?

as I think about seizing the heavens
a fly whirls around and around in this
room.

I been working on the railroad . . .

the Great Editor said he wanted to meet me
in person before he published my book.
he said most writers were sons of bitches
and that he just didn't want to print anybody
who was
so since he paid the train fare
I went on down there to
New Orleans
where I lived around the corner from him
in a small room.

the Great Editor lived in a cellar with a
printing press, his wife and two
dogs.
the Great Editor also published a famous
literary magazine
but my projected book
would be his first try at
that.
he survived on the magazine, on luck, on
handouts.

each night I ate dinner with the Great
Editor and his wife (my only meal and
probably theirs too).
then we'd drink beer until midnight
when I'd go to my small room
open a bottle of wine and begin
typing.
he said he didn't have enough
poems.
"I need more poems," he said.

he had caught up on my back poems
and as I wrote the new poems he
printed them.
I was writing directly into the
press.

around noon each day I'd go around
the corner
knock on the window
and see the Great Editor
feeding pages of my poems
into the press.

the Great Editor was also the Great
Publisher, the Great Printer and a
many Great Number of Other Things,
and I was practically the unknown
poet so it was all quite
strange.

anyhow, I would wave the pages at
him and he would stop the press
and let me in.
he'd sit and read the poems:
"hmmm . . . good . . . why don't you
come to dinner tonight?"
then I'd leave.

some noons I'd knock on the
window
without any poems
and the Great Editor would stare
at me as if I were a
giant roach.
he wouldn't open the door.

"GO AWAY!" I could hear him scream
through the window, "GO AWAY AND
DON'T COME BACK UNTIL YOU HAVE
SOME POEMS!"

he would be genuinely angry
and it puzzled me: he expected
4 or 5 poems from me
each day.

I'd stop somewhere for a couple of
six-packs
go back to my room
and begin to type.
the afternoon beer always tasted

good and I'd come up with
some poems . . .

take them back
knock on the window
wave the pages.

the Great Editor would smile
pleasantly
open the door
take the pages
sit down and read them:
"umm . . . ummm . . . these are
good . . . why don't you drop by
for dinner tonight?"

and in between the afternoon
and the evening
I'd go back to my room
and sign more and more
colophons.
the pages were thick, heavily
grained, expensive,
designed to last
2,000 years.
the signings were slow and
laborious
written out with a special
pen . . .
thousands of colophons
and as I got drunker
to keep from going

altogether crazy
I began making drawings
and
statements . . .
when I finished signing the
colos
the stack of pages stood
six feet tall
in the center of the
room.

as I said,
it was a very strange time
for an unknown writer.
he said it to me one
night:
"Chinaski, you've ruined
poetry for me . . . since I've
read you I just can't read
anything else . . ."

high praise, indeed, but I
knew what he meant.

each day his wife stood
on the street corners
trying to sell paintings,
her paintings and the paintings
of other painters.
she was a beautiful and
fiery woman.

finally, the book was done.
that is, except for the binding;
the Great Editor couldn't do
the binding, he had to pay for
the binding part and that
pissed him.

but our job was done,
his and mine,
and the Great Editor and
his wife put me on the train
back to L.A.

both of them standing there
on the platform
looking at me and smiling
as I looked back from my
seat by the window.
it was . . .
embarrassing . . .

finally the train started
to slowly roll
and I waved and they
waved
and then as I was
nearly out of sight
the Great Editor
jumped up and down
like a little boy,
still waving . . .

I walked back to the bar
car and decided to stay
my trip
there.

it was some stops and
some hours later
when the porter came
back there:
"HENRY CHINASKI! IS THERE
A HENRY CHINASKI HERE?"

"here my good man,"
I said.

"damn, man," he said, "I've
been looking all *over* this
train for you!"

I tipped him and opened the
telegram:
"YOU'RE STILL A S.O.B. BUT
WE STILL LOVE YOU . . .
      Jon and Louise . . ."

I motioned the porter over
ordered a double scotch
on the rocks
then I had it
and I held it up a moment
toasted them an almost

lyrical blessing
then drank it down
as the train
rolled and swayed
swayed and rolled
working me further and further
away
from those magic
people.

the way it goes

he died one Sunday afternoon
and the funeral was on a Wednesday;
the crowd was small: his wife, his
sons, related family members, a couple
of screenwriters plus 3 or 4 others;
he was discovered by H. L. Mencken
in the 30's;
he wrote a clear simple line
a passionate line,
fine short stories and novels;
he was stricken late in life,
became blind, had both legs
amputated, and they kept cutting
at him, operating again and
again.

in the hospital
he stayed in that bed for years;
he had to be turned, fed, bed-
panned,
but while there
he dictated a total new novel
to his wife.

he never quit: that novel was
published.

one day when I was visiting
him
he told me, "you know, Hank,
when I was all right, I had all
these friends, then . . . when this
happened, they dropped me, it was
like I had leprosy . . ."

and he smiled.

there was a breeze moving through
the window
and there he was
the sunlight moving
half across him.

those friends didn't
deserve him.

a great writer
and a greater human.

John, the crowd will never have
the love of the few—
as if I would have to tell
you.

alone in a time of armies

I was 22 in that roominghouse in Philadelphia and I was starving and
mad in a prosperous world at war
and one night sitting at my window I saw in the room across the
way in another Philadelphia roominghouse
a young lady grab a young man and kiss him with great joy and
passion.
it was then that I realized the depraved corner I had worked myself
into:
I wanted to be that young man at that moment
but I didn't want to do the many things he had probably done to get
where he had arrived.
yet worse, I realized that I could be wrong.
I left my room and began walking the streets.
I kept walking even though I had not eaten that
day.
(the day has eaten you! sang the chorus)
I walked, I walked.
I must have walked 5 miles, then I
returned.
the lights in the room across the way were
out.
mine were too.

I undressed and went to bed.
I didn't want to be what they wanted me to
be.
and then
like them
I slept.

going modern

I drank more than usual tonight, got some writing out of
it but here I had this IBM electric typewriter and both
tapes ran out at once: the typing tape and the erasing tape
and I can usually replace these
but tonight I was too drunk:

it was a battle of the soul to get the typing tape in but
when it came to the erasing tape I ran out of
soul: the sticky strip stuck against things it
shouldn't, it twisted pretzel-like and I threw it out and
tried another.
it must have been ten minutes before I got it
right.
meanwhile—I got into another bottle, then I looked down at
the box on the floor: I was down to one typing tape and one
erasing tape so I went to the Instruction Booklet and dialed the
800 number which I think was in Maryland or South Dakota and
was surprised to get an answer: it was 3:30 A.M. in
Los Angeles.

I told the lady what I needed but she didn't quite understand,
she kept demanding an order #.

I had Richard Wagner on full bombast on the radio and I told her
that I didn't *have* a god damned order #.
she
hung up on me and I dialed again and this time I got a nice young
man and he said, "that's great music you're listening to . . ." but
the nice young man also demanded an order #.
I drained off a full glass of wine, said, "listen, I didn't have an
order # the first time I phoned . . ."

"but, sir, the second time you phone the rule is that you must have
an order #."

"you mean, I can't get my tapes? I'm a fucking writer, how am I
going to make it? would you cut the horns off a bull?"

"do you have your last bill before you,
sir?"

"yes, yes . . ."

"the order # must be on the bill,
sir . . ."

"I tell you, there's nothing here to indicate an order
#!"

"well, sir . . ."

"NO, NO, NO!"

I drained another glass of
wine, "listen, let's *pretend* that this is the *first* time I've *ever* phoned
you and let's begin at the beginning?"

"all right, sir . . . now, *can* you read me off what you
wish?"

"thank YOU! I want 18 lift off tapes, item # 1136433 and I want 12
cassettes, black, item # 1299508."

then I read him off my American Express card # which I won't
                                                            include
here.

"you'll have all your materials within 8 to ten days, sir . . ."

"THANK YOU!"

then, as I hung up, I noticed a line on my past bill, it said ORDER
NUMBER 11101—this and that and dash this and that.
it had been there all the
time.

NOW I was READY to type again, help was on the way, my mind was
free, I leaned a bit forward and began to type:
frsyj mrbrt ,syyrtrf sd ,ivj sd yjsy dytuhhlr yo dysy
slibr s,pmh yjr %rp%;r smf om d%oyr pg yjs
%rp%;r.
frsyj eo%% mr yjr rsdody %sty.

it doesn't always work

I knew a writer once
who always tried to tighten his lines

like he'd write:
an old man in a green felt hat walked down the
street.

change to:
old man in green walked down street.

change to:
old green man walked street.

change to:
green man walked.

change to:
green walked.

finally this writer said,
shit, I can't fart,

and he blew his brains
out.

blew brains out.

blew brains.

blew.

I have this room

I have this room up here where I sit alone and it's much
like my rooms of the past—bottles and papers, books,
belts, combs, old newspapers, various trash spread about.
my disorder was never chosen, it just arrived and it
stayed.

in the time of each there's never enough time to place
all things right—there is always breakdown, loss, the
hard mathematic of
confusion and
weariness.
we are harangued with immense and trivial tasks
and times arrive of stoicism or of horror when it becomes
impossible to pay a gas bill or to even answer the threat
from the IRS or termites or the papal doom of serving
your soul up for self-surveillance.

I have this room up here and it's much the same as always:
the failure to live grandly with the female or the
universe, it gets so stuffy, all rubbed raw with self-
complaint, attrition, re-
runs.

I have this room up here and I've had this same room in
so many cities—the years shot suddenly away, I still
sit feeling no different than in my youth.

the room always was—still is—best at night—
the yellowness of the electric light while sitting and
drinking—all we've ever needed was a minor retreat
from all the galling nonsense:
we could always handle the worst if we were sometimes
allowed the tiniest of awakenings from the nightmare,
and the gods, so far, have allowed us
this.

I have this room up here and I sit alone in the floating,
poking, crazy ultimates, I am lazy in these fields of pain
and my friends, the walls, embrace this once-gamble—
my heart can't laugh but sometimes it smiles
in the yellow electric light: to have come so far to
sit alone
again
in this room up here.

a man for the centuries

all in all, drinking here into the early morning hours and
taking what the radio gives me: many of the composers of
the ages have entered, have left, but all in all, sucking at this
lovely wine and listening, I have come up with Bach: he
tastes the laughter of joy before death, each note like a wild
bean, I am saddened that he braced his life with God,
although I understand that this is sometimes necessary, but
it's not so much what a man believes as what he does and
Bach did it so well, listening to him in this small room he
makes me feel like a hero just to be alive, to have arms, legs,
a head, all the various parts as I sit listening, ingesting the
sound while sucking at this lovely wine

a dead man has become such a friend

I hope he found God
he deserves God
and God
if He is there
deserves
Bach

and we do too:

we winos
we agnostics:

those notes jumping like wild
beans.

dear old dad

one of the most fortunate things
to have happened to me
was to have a cruel and sadistic
father.

after him
the worst things that the Fates
have thrown upon me
have hardly seemed as
terrible—
things that would cause other
men
anger, despair, disgust,
madness, thoughts of suicide
and
so forth
have only had a minor effect
upon me
due to my
upbringing:
after my father
almost *anything* else looked
good.

I should really be
thankful to that
old fuck
so long dead
now
he readied me
for all the numerous
hells
by getting me there
early
on time
through the inescapable
years.

peace and love

back in the 60's
I wrote a column for a hippie
newspaper.

I wasn't a hippie (I was in
my 40's) but I thought it was
nice of the paper
to allow me to state my
errant
views
once a
week.

for each of these works of
genius
I was given
$10 (sometimes).

now
there was another hippie
newspaper
bidding for my
services.

they were offering me
$15 for each
column.

not wanting to appear
the deserter
I was asking for
$20.

so
I was over at the other
paper
quite often
haggling with the
editor
about the 5-buck
difference
over a couple of
6-packs.

nice thing about that
hippie paper
when I walked in
everybody started
hollering my
name:

"Hey, Chinaski!"

"Chinaski!"

I liked that, it
made me feel like a
star.

and they also
hollered,
"PEACE AND LOVE!"

"PEACE AND LOVE!"

lots of young little chicks
hollered this at
me
and I liked
that
although I never
returned the
salutations
except for a slight
smile
and an almost
invisible
wave of the left
hand

to go in to see the
editor and tell
him, "listen, nice place
you've got here, we've got to
work something
out . . ."

yet
we couldn't seem
to
but I decided to
keep working at
it . . .

so,
there was this one week
when I walked down
there
and the whole place was
closed down: nobody, no-
thing
in
there . . .

well, I thought, maybe they
moved, maybe they found
a
cheaper place.

so
I moved away from there
and walked along
and as I did
I looked into this cafe
and the strangest of
longshots
occurred:

there was the editor
sitting at this
table
so
I walked in
and he saw me
coming up
and said, "sit down,
Chinaski."

I did
and asked
him:

"what happened?"

"it's sad, we had to
fold just when we were
picking up on circulation
and
ads."

"yeah? and?"

"well, 4 or 5 of them
had no place to stay so
I told them they could
stay at the office at
night as long as they kept
it quiet and dark . . . so
they brought in their water
beds, their pipes, their acid,

their guitars, their grass, their
Bobby Dylan albums and
it seemed all
right . . ."

"yeah? and?? . . ."

"they used the telephones at
night. long distance to many places,
some of them like
France, India and China
but
most of them
were
U.S. based
but wherever they called
it was always for a long
time, anywhere between 45
minutes and 3 and one-half
hours . . ."

"Christ . . ."

"yeah, we couldn't pay the bill,
hence no phones, collection agency
after us, we had to
fold . . ."

"sorry, man . . ."

"it's all
right . . ."

"I've got a little bit of
green," I told him, "let's
go find a
bar . . ."

well, we found
one and he ordered a
scotch and soda and I
ordered a whiskey
sour
and we sat there
looking straight
forward
really
not much to
say

except
some time later
still sitting there
drinking about the
same

he told me
his wife had left
him
for a real estate
agent
who worked out of
Arizona and

New Mexico
where things were
going
especially good
mostly around
Santa
Fe.

the world of valets

_____

after having my car broken into twice
at the track—
you know how it is: your door is
jammed open when you
arrive
and inside there is nothing but
large empty holes where the
equipment was, nothing but the
curling of the
wires . . .

so I decided upon valet
parking
feeling it would be cheaper in
the long
run . . .

and the first thing I noticed
my first day at valet
parking
was that for the extra
price
they threw in a little
conversation

"hey, buddy, how'd you get a
car like that? you don't look like
a guy with brains . . . you must have
inherited some money from your
father . . ."

"you guessed it," I told the
valet.

the next day another valet
told me, "listen, I can get you
some cheap wine by the case and there's
a crippled girl in the motel across the
track that gives the best head since
Cleopatra . . ."

the next one said, "hey, fuck-face,
how's it going?"

I watched and noticed that the
valets treated the other patrons with
standard civility.

then
one day
they wouldn't even give me
a ticket tab for my
car.

"how am I going to prove this
car is
mine?"

"you'll just have to
convince us . . ."

when I came out that
evening
there was my car
parked at a little getaway
lane by the
hedge, I didn't have to
wait like the
others
and I'd always hear some
little
story:

"hey, man, my wife tried to
commit suicide . . ."

"I can understand
that . . ."

day after day
a different story from a
different
valet:

"I love my wife but I got this
girlfriend and I fuck the shit out of
her . . . I mean, one day all I'm going to be
doing is shooting blue smoke, so what the
fuck?"

"Frank," I told him, "how you run out your
string is up to you . . ."

and
like say
last Wednesday there was an odd
occurrence:

there's the head valet
and he has these headphones and
mike
he used to call the cars of the
patrons
to the out-riding pick-
up drivers
and he placed the headphones
on my dome and there was
the mike
and he told me,
"Frank wants to hear from
you . . ."

and I saw him out there
tooling the white
pick-up

and I spoke into the
mike:

"Frank, baby, everything is
death!"

and I heard him back through the
headphones:

"FUCKING A-RIGHT!"

he waved and then had to
slam on the brakes
almost hitting a blue
'86 Caddy

it was the Hollywood Park meeting
summer 1986
and the valets who parked the
old man's battered 1979
BMW with the fog lights ripped
away
and the small colors of the
German flag
left corner
back window

I got into that machine and drove it
out of there, the centuries still
moving toward the dark

forever and
forever
and I drove east down Century
got on the Harbor Freeway
south

there's much more to betting the
horses than cashing or tearing up
tickets.

I live to write and now I'm dying

I've told this one before and it has never gotten published so
maybe I didn't tell it properly, so
it goes like this: I was in Atlanta, living in a paper
shack for $1.25 a week.
no light.
no heat.
it's freezing, I'm out of money but I do have
stamps
envelopes
paper.

I mail out letters for help, only I don't know
anybody.
there are my parents but I know they won't
care.
I write one to them
anyhow.

then
who else?

the editor of the *New Yorker,* he must know me, I've
mailed him a story a week for
years.

and the editor of *Esquire*

and the *Atlantic Monthly*

and *Harper's*.

"this is not a submission," I wrote
them, "or maybe it is . . . anyhow . . ."
and then came the pitch: "just a dollar, it will
save my life . . ." and etc. and etc. . . .

and somehow
I had the addresses of Kay Boyle and Caresse
Crosby
and
I wrote them.

at least Caresse *had* published me in her
Portfolio. . . .

I took all the letters down to the corner mailbox
dropped them in and
waited.

I thought, somebody will take pity on the starving
writer, I am a *dedicated*
man:

I live to write and now I am
dying.

and
each day
I thought that I
would.

I stalled the rent, I found pieces of food
in the streets, usually
frozen.
I had to take it in and thaw it
under my bedcover.

I thought of Hamsun's *Hunger*
and I
laughed.

day followed cold day,
slowly.

the first letter was from my father,
a six pager, and I shook the pages
again and again
but there was no
money
just
advice,
the main bit
being: "you will never be a
writer! what you write is too
ugly! *nobody* wants to read that
CRAP!"

then the day
came!
a letter from Caresse
Crosby!

I opened it.
no money
but
neatly typed:
"Dear Charles:
it was good to hear from
you. I have given up the
magazine. I now live in a
castle in Italy. it is
high on a mountain but
below me is a village
and I often go down there
to help the poor. I feel
it is my calling.
      love,
         Caresse . . ."

didn't she read my letter?
I
was the poor!
did I have to be an Italian
peasant to
qualify?

and the magazine editors never
responded and neither did
Kay Boyle
but I never liked her writing
anyhow.
and I never expected much
from the magazine
editors.

but Caresse
Crosby?
BLACK SUN PRESS?

I now even remember how
I finally got out of
Atlanta.
I was just wandering the
streets and I got to this
little wooded
area.
there was a tin shack there
and a big red sign
said: "HELP WANTED!"

inside was a man with
pleasant blue eyes and he was
quite friendly
and I signed on to a
railroad track gang:
"someplace west of
Sacramento."

on the ride back
in that dusty one-hundred-year-old coach with
the torn seats and the rats and
the cans of pork and beans
none of the fellows knew that I had been
published in *Portfolio* along with
Sartre, Henry Miller, Genet and
etc.
along with reproduced paintings by
Picasso and etc. and etc.
and if they had known they wouldn't have
given a shit
and frankly
I didn't either.

it was only some decades after
when I was in *slightly* better circumstances
I happened to read about the death of
Caresse Crosby
and I once again became confounded
by her refusal to
send a lousy buck to a
starving American genius.

that's it
this is the last time I'm writing this
one.
it should get
published . . .

and if it does I'm going to get hundreds
of letters
from starving American geniuses
asking for a buck, five bucks, ten or
more.

I won't tell them I'm helping the
poor, à la Caresse.

I'll tell them to read
the *Collected Poems of
Kay Boyle*.

rip it

---

when a poem doesn't work, forget it, don't hound it, don't
fondle it and molest it, don't make it join the A.A. or
become a Born Again
Christian.

when a poem doesn't work, just pull the sheet out of the
machine, rip it, toss it in the basket—that feels
good.

listen, you write because it's the last machinegun
on the last hill.

you write because you're a bird sitting on a wire, then
suddenly your wings flap and your little dumb ass is
up in the air.

you write because the madhouse sits there belching and
farting, heavy with minds and bodies, you write because
you fear ultimate madness . . .

when a poem doesn't work, it doesn't work; forget it;
pace is the essence.

I know of a lady who writes so many poems that she must
arise at 7 A.M. and type until midnight.
she is in a poetry writing competition—with
herself.

when a poem doesn't work, it's not the end; it's not even a
rotten banana, it's not even a wrong number call asking for
Blanche Higgins.

when a poem doesn't work it is just because you didn't have
it that time.
or have it
at any time?

take that paper, tear it, basket it, then
wait.

but don't sit in front of the machine, do something
else—watch tv, say hello to your wife, pet the
cat.

everything is not made
of paper.

Henry Miller and Burroughs

you mean, you don't like them?
I am asked again and
again.

no.

what is it?

just don't like.

I can't believe this. why
don't you like
them?

oh, god, crap off.

you like anybody?

sure.

name them.

Celine, Turgenev, Dostoevsky, early
Gorky, J. D. Salinger, e. e. cummings,
Jeffers, Sherwood Anderson, Li Po,
Pound, Carson McCullers . . .

o.k., o.k., but I can't believe you
don't like Henry Miller or Burroughs,
especially, Henry Miller.

crap off.

ever met Miller?

no.

I think you are kidding me about not liking
Henry Miller.

uh uh.

is it professional jealousy?

I don't think so.

Miller opened doors for all of
us.

and I am opening my door for
you.

why are you upset with all
this?

not upset, but you ever fucked a
chicken in the ass?

no.

go do it, then come back and we'll
talk about William B. and especially
Henry M.

I think you're a weird prick . . .

move out or I'll punch you
out.

you'll hear from me.

if you're ever heard from it will
be because I write of
you, now move
out!

good night.

good, I said as the door
closed,
night.

family tree

not much in my family tree, well, there was my uncle
John, wanted by the F.B.I., they got me first.
Grandpa Leonard, on my father's side, he became very
kind when drunk, praised everybody, gave away money,
wept copiously for the human condition, but when he
sobered up was said to be one of the meanest
creatures ever seen, heard or avoided.
not much else except Grandpa Willy on my mother's
side (over there in Germany): "He was a kind man,
Henry, but all he wanted to do was drink and play his
violin, he played it so very good, he had this fine
position with this leading symphony orchestra but he
lost that because of his drinking, nobody would hire
him, but he was good with the violin, he went to cafes
and got a table and played his violin, he put his hat
on the table upside down and the people would put so
much money in there but he kept buying drinks and
playing the violin and soon he didn't play so good
anymore and they would ask him to leave but the next
night he would find another cafe, another table, he
wrote his own music and nobody could play the violin
like he could.
He died one night at his table, he put the violin
down, had a drink, placed his head on the table and
died."

212

well, there was my uncle Ben, he was so handsome it
was frightening, he was too handsome, he just radiated,
you couldn't believe it and it wouldn't go away, all he
could do about it was smile and light another cigarette
and find another woman to support and console him, and
then find another woman to do the same, and then find
another.
he died of TB in a sanitarium in the hills, the pack of
cigarettes under his pillow, dead he smiled, and at his
funeral 2 dozen of the most beautiful women in Pasadena,
Glendale and Echo Park wept
unashamedly as my father cursed him in his coffin: "You
rotten son of a bitch, you never worked a day in your
life!"

my father, of course, was one I could never figure out—
I mean, how he could have ever gotten into the family
tree.
but I was feeling pretty good up to here, there's hardly
any use making this a depressing poem.

well, sometimes you get a strange monkey on a branch and all you
can do is forgive if you can and forget it, if possible,
and if neither of these works, then think of the others
and know that, at least, some of your blood is not without
hope.

being here

when it gets at its worst, there is nothing to be
done, it's almost to laugh, putting your clothes
on again, going out, seeing faces, machines,
streets, buildings, the unfurling of the
world.

I act out motions, exchange monies, answer
questions, ask few, as the hours toil on,
following me, they are not always constantly
terrible—at times I am stricken with a wild
joy and I laugh, hardly knowing
why.

perhaps the worst trick that I have learned is to
endure; I must learn to give way, that is not a
suspicious thing.

we are far too serious, we must learn to juggle
our heavens and our hells—the game is playing
us, we must play back.

our shoes walk along, carrying
us.

when it gets at its worst, nothing should be
done.

the exactitude is the freedom: one hundred
thousand walls or more
and more
of nothingness, your bones know more than your
mind.

the only life

I was like one of those nuts from centuries past, I was
Romantically mad with my fixation—ha, ha, to be a
writer, I wrote night and day. I even wrote when I was
asleep
and most often I wrote when I was drunk, even when I
wasn't writing.

ah, those dozens of cheap rooms, my belly flattened to
my asshole, I became 133 pounds on a 6 foot
frame. I STARVED. haha, so I could write.
(this is a true story) (aren't they all?) and
all my writings came back and I finally had to
throw them away because
there was more space of paper than there was space of
me
and I continued to write new works which continued to
come back and I thought
Schopenhauer, Van Gogh, Shostakovich, Céline, Dos-
toevsky
and I continued to write and it came back
again
and I thought
Villon, Gorky, Turgenev, Sherwood Anderson
and I wrote and wrote

and still nothing happened
and when I finally did EAT
you have no idea how
BEAUTIFUL FOOD CAN TRULY BE, EACH BITE LIKE A MIRACLE OF
SUNLIGHT TO THE STAGGERING SOUL, haha,
and I thought,
Hamsun, Ezra Pound, T. S. Eliot
but nothing happened—
all my typewriters to hock and gone I
printed the pages in ink
and they came back
and I threw them away
and wrote some more and starved some
more.

oh, I had an apprenticeship, I did, and now I've had a bit of
luck, some are beginning to think that I can write, but
actually only the writing is the thing, now as it was then,
whether yes or no or in between, it's only the writing, it's
the only go when all else says stop
and some of it still comes back now and I think
Nietzsche, e. e. cummings, Robinson Jeffers, Sartre, Camus,
                                        Hemingway
the sound of the machine, the sound of the machine, words
biting into paper, there is nothing else, there can be nothing
else, whether it comes back, whether it stays and when
it ends, ha
ha.

Charles Bukowski
1148 W. Santa Cruz st.
San Pedro, Calif. 90731

        Stomping at the Savoy

now look, Captain, I want the walking wounded at
their posts, we can't spare a man, if these
Huns knew our ranks were thinning they'd
eat us alive and rape our women and children
and, god help us, our pets
too!

out of water? have them drink their blood!
what do you think this is, a fucking
picnic?
I'll give you your picnic up your
ARSE! get
that?

now look... we lure them in, outflank them,
they'll be gobblin' their own shit in
panic!
we'll have their bones for picket fences!
you'll be heroes to our ladies, they'll
lick your balls gratefully into Eternity!
got that?

quitters don't win, and besides that, any
man I see retreating, I'm gonna blow a hole
in him big enough so you'll be able to see
your grandmother's asshole picking dasies in
Petaluma!
hear me?

oh shit! I BEEN HIT! get the doc! get all
the docs!
cocksucker! whoda guessed? lucky shot!
those Huns couldn't hit a wet dream at
3 paces!

Captain! you're in command! you blow this
thing and I'm gonna twist your legs and stuff
'em up your stupid rear! got it?

I con't want those Huns finger-fucking Melba
on the veranda!
God's on our side! He told me once, "Listen,
those Huns gotta go! they don't wash under
the armpits and they comb their hair with
peach jelly!"

Captain! I think !'m going! get a nurse
here, I need some head! and hurry! this
war ain't got all day!

                                    3-4-90

stomping at the Savoy

now look, Captain, I want the walking wounded at
their posts, we can't spare a man, if these
Huns knew our ranks were thinning they'd
eat us alive and rape our women and children
and, god help us, our pets
too!

out of water? have them drink their blood!
what do you think this is, a fucking
picnic?
I'll give you your *picnic* up your
ARSE! get
that?

now look . . . we lure them in, outflank them,
they'll be gobblin' their own shit in
panic!
we'll have their bones for picket fences!
you'll be heroes to our ladies, they'll
lick your balls gratefully into Eternity!
got that?

quitters don't win, and besides that, any
man I see retreating, I'm gonna blow a hole
in him big enough so you'll be able to see

your grandmother's asshole picking daisies in
Petaluma!
hear me?

oh shit! I BEEN HIT! get the doc! get all
the docs!
cocksucker! whoda guessed? lucky shot!
those Huns couldn't hit a wet dream at
3 paces!

Captain! you're in command! you blow this
thing and I'm gonna twist your legs and stuff
'em up your stupid rear! got it?

I don't want those Huns finger-fucking Melba
on the veranda!
God's on our side! He told me once, "Listen,
those Huns gotta go! they don't wash under
the armpits and they comb their hair with
peach jelly!"

Captain! I think I'm going! get a nurse
here, I need some head! and hurry! this
war ain't got all day!

the glory days

the dead rivers run backwards into nowhere,
the fish cry through neon memories,
and I remember you drunk in bed
in that cheap hotel room
with nobody to live with but me,
what a trundling hell that must have
been, you with
a young sot ten years your junior
pacing the floor in his shorts while
bragging to the deaf gods while
smashing glasses against the walls.

you were certainly caught out of place and
time,
your marriage broken on stained
tiles
and you
being humped by a
bewhiskered jerk who was terrorized by
life, beaten by the odds, this
thing
pacing the floor, rolled wet cigarette
in monkey mouth, then
stopping to
open another bottle of cheap
wine.

the dead rivers of our lives,
hearts like rocks.

pour the red blood of wine.
curse, complain, wail, sing
in that cheap hotel room.

you, awakening . . . "Hank?"
"yeh . . . here . . . what the fuck you
want?"
"hell, gimme a drink . . ."

the waste
yet the courage of the
gamble.

where's the rent due coming from?

I'll get a job.
you'll get a job.
yeah, fat chance. fat shit
chance
anyhow, enough wine gets you past
thinking.

I break a large drinking glass against the
wall.
the phone rings.
it's the desk clerk again:
"Mr. Chinaski, I must warn you . . ."

"AH, GO WARN YOUR MOTHER'S CUNT!"

the slamming of the phone.
power.

I am a man.
you like me, you like that.
and, I've got brains too, I've always
told you that.

"Hank?"
"yeh?"
"how many bottles we got left?"
"3."
"good."

pacing the floor, looking to fly, looking
to live.
neon memories cry the fish.

4th floor of a 6th street hotel, windows
open to the city of hell, the precious breathing
of the lonely pigeons.

you drunk in bed, me playing at miracle,
wine-bottle corks and full ashtrays.
it's like everybody's dead, everybody's
dead with their heads on,
we've got to conquer the flailing of
nowhere.

look at me in undershirt and shorts,
bare feet bleeding shards of glass.

there's some way out that begins with
3 bottles
left.

congrats, Chinaski

as I near 70
I get letters, cards, little gifts
from strange people.
congratulations, they tell
me,
congratulations.

I know what they mean:
the way I have lived
I should have been dead in half
that time.

I have piled myself with a mass of
grand abuse, been
careless toward myself
almost to the point of
madness,
I am still here
leaning toward this machine
in this smoke-filled room,
this large blue trashcan to my
left
full of empty
containers.

the doctors have no answers
and the gods are
silent.

congratulations, death,
on your patience.
I have helped you all that
I can.

now one more poem
and a walk out on the balcony,
such a fine night there.

I am dressed in shorts and stockings,
gently scratch my old
belly,
look out there
look off there
where dark meets dark

it's been one hell of a crazy
ball game.

he went for the windmills, yes

something to keep you going is needed
badly
as the milkmaids now scream obscenities
in sundry dialects,
the mill is shut down,
there are mass murders at hamburger
joints,
friar Tuck is screwed,
the United States ranks 17th of the
nations in longevity of the
individual,
and nobody wipes the windshield.

the beast sleeps in Beverly Hills,
Van Gogh is an absentee billionaire,
the Man from Mars deals the ace of
spades,
Hollywood goes soap opera,
the horse rides the jock,
the whore blows congress,
the cat is down to one life,
the dead end street is a psychiatrist,
the table is set with fish-head fantasies,
the dream strikes like a blackjack in the men's
crapper,
the homeless are rolled,

the dice are fixed,
the curtain is down,
the seats are empty,
the watchman has suicided,
the lights are out,
nobody waits for Godot
something to keep you going is needed
badly,
madly,
right now
in the burning forest
in the dying sea
in the dull sonnets
and the wasted
sunrises,
something is needed
here
besides this rotten
music,
these shorn decades,
this place like this,
this time,
yours,
mutilated, spit
away,
a mirror's back, a
hog's teat;
a seed upon a rock,
cold,
not even the death of
a cockroach
now.

all my friends

Van Gogh just walked in and complained to me
that Theo had sent him the wrong
paints.
he was gone no longer than a moment
when Dostoevsky knocked and asked for a
loan to play the roulette wheel,
claimed he was working on a masterpiece,
something called *Crime and Punishment*
then Chatterton knocked and asked if I might
have some rat poison, said he had an idea of
how to get away from the rats.
Villon sat around bitching half the night about
how he had been barred from Paris—not for his
writings but simply because of some petty
thievery, really, he said, a chickenshit deal.
then Ernie came in, he was drunk, and he started
talking about the bullfights, that's all he talks about:
the bullfights and fishing, the BIG one that got away,
and he's always on the war, the war, the war.
I was glad when he left.
Picasso came in then and complained that his
shack job, who was also a painter, was jealous of
him, she thought she could paint but was being

held back because she was a woman and that some
day she would paint a book about him calling him a
petty jerk-off monster and from this she would gain
the only fame which she thirsted so badly for.
then Knut Hamsun came in and claimed he was
framed in the war crimes deal.
followed by Ezra who spoke of the same thing.
followed by the good doctor, Céline.
then H.D. came in and said, "I only wish now that I
had used my real name, Hilda Doolittle, to hell with
the Imagist Manifesto, it ended up anyhow that when
people saw 'H.D.,' all they did was reverse the initials
and think of that fucker, D. H. Lawrence."
then Mozart, the x-child prodigy knocked and asked
for a nickel, I gave it to him, what a fake pretending to be
in trouble after writing more symphonies than any man
I can ever remember.
then there was Ernie again, asking to borrow a shot gun
shell, claiming he had a special game in
mind.
I let him have it.

then Borodin knocked, claiming his wife made him sleep on
the stairway and always raised hell when he pressed his teabag
with a spoon.

after that I got tired of all the knocks and all the people—I kept
screaming at Beethoven to go away but he kept knocking—
so I cut the lights, stuck in my earplugs and went to sleep
but it was no good because I had this nightmare and here was
this Van Gogh fellow again, only he had not only cut off one ear

but both ears, I mean, he really looked frigged-over, and he sent
one ear to one prostitute and the other to another and the first
prostitute gagged and tossed the ear over her left shoulder but
the second prostitute just laughed, pulled down her panties and
chugged the ear up her rectum saying, "now I can hear the pricks
entering and the shit dropping."

then I awakened and Hemingway's skull bones and blood dripped
down on me from the
ceiling.

a reader writes

"Dear Mr. Chinaski:
I still like your writing but I liked it
better back then, I mean when you were
writing things like, 'when she bent over I
saw all that ass.' Or
you wrote about the drunk tanks and the rats
and the roaches and the mice.
I liked all your troubles with women, I have
troubles with women too and I really dug what
you were getting at.
I liked all the craziness, the back alley
fights, the police raids.
Let's have more of this, it keeps me going.
I know it won't mean shit to you but I'm
going to tell you, anyhow.
There's a group of us and we get oiled, we
put on Frank Sinatra records and read your stuff
out loud.
Give us some more of the old
stuff.
yeah, yeah!"

Dear Reader:
About Mr. Sinatra, let's forget that, but I
must tell you that I am now 70 years old and it's
a surprise to me too but if I went on writing about
peeking up women's asses I wouldn't have time to
write about how my cat walks across the floor while
carrying the secrets of Eternity to my brain, I mean,
look, you can write something to death, most do when
they find it sells books but I don't write to sell
books I write to keep my psyche's guts from drowning
in the dung-filled waters of this so-called Existence.
Take Hemingway, he wrote himself into the same tight
circle which eventually closed and squeezed him to
death.
Take J. D. Salinger, he wrote lively and compelling
tales of ethyl youth but when he grew older there
was no such thing left to write about.
Specialization is death, bad rotten candy.
Gamble is the only out, you have to keep throwing
new dice.
On women, they are over-rated because we over-rate
them.
You really can't expect me to go on writing about the
big asses of some women.
But I did have some problems, a few doubts about
leaving this vast and lucrative area—for I was getting
more than the rent by doing so and so why take a chance
about writing about, say, a one-winged bluebird struggling
in a stack of mulch?
I had to, that's why, and take away the rent and more,
and I'll still have to.

I make no excuses for my subject matter and it makes no
excuses for me.
Like, I once knew a popular song writer who had a
problem—he had gotten famous by writing down and out
songs about life in Hollywood motels and he lived in
this one and got rich and famous and he still kept
living there, afraid that if he left that place he'd
lose his persona and his popularity.
But actually, it makes no sense for a rich man to be
living in a cheap Hollywood motel because it just
isn't the same as a poor man living there.
Luckily for him they closed the place down and he
didn't have to pretend anymore.
Like my stories about cheap roominghouses were
written because I lived there.
We move on and if we're lucky we find new
material.
Wonderment, newness and hell are everywhere.
Frank Sinatra sings his same old songs over and over
again.
That's because he's locked in with what made him
famous.
Fame has nothing to do with anything.
Moving on has.
I'll be dying soon, that's nothing extraordinary
but I won't be able to write about it
and I'll be glad that I didn't go on writing about
what you find to be interesting and I do
not.
Christ, man, I don't mean to get so holy about
all this, there's nothing holy about writing

but it is the greatest drunken enactment that I
know of.
It was then and it is now.
Women's asses and everything else.
I'm laughing at the darkness just like you are.
Next time you boys get oiled, put on some
Sibelius.

        sure,
              Henry Chinaski

ow said the cow to the fence that linked

, flounce those asshole babies,
the lepers are drunk on coconut
milk
, the pervert's last dream was of
bacon mixed with rump
pie
, dead is dead enough
red is red enough
and the horse failed in the
queen's face
and an hour later
she had his balls in her hands
and his head mounted between
the motorcycle handles of
Hades
, the green forests in my mind
are blind
as I reach for the toilet paper
roll
the world barks once and
vanishes
, vanilla, vanilla, vanilla,
imagine yourself in Prokofiev's
rear pocket during a summer

squall outside the villa of a
vermouth drinking dog-
eater
, Paris is a place outside of
nowhere that used to
be
, keep getting phone calls
from totally mad people who
love me because they believe
my madness justifies theirs
which is worse than very low
grade
, pain is like a rocket, get enough
of it
and it will shoot you through
and past all nonsense
for a while
only
, the lady brought me a drink
and I brought the lady a drink
and the lady brought me a
drink
and then I brought the lady a
drink
and then the bartender
plucked out his left eye
stuck it into his mouth and
blew it to the ceiling
as a guy walked through the
door and asked,
"Is Godot in here?"
, the placenta is the hymn of

the forgotten wound
and don't you owe me 20
bucks which I lent you during
the
Mardi Gras?
, o, damn all things and
birds and lakes and garter
belts
o, why are we so stuffed
with helium crap?
o, who stole the eyes
and put the bottle caps on
Georgia's ass?

, why does the door open
backwards?

, hey, this stale breathing of
the stinking drums . . .
wherein come these arms?
catch that drunken lark!

, that pettifog of perfection . . .
that pellucid yawn of
burning . . .

, Christ stopped short,
the tire blew,
I opened the trunk and
the jack was
missing.

my America, 1936

you've got no get up and go,
said my father,
you know how much money
it took me to raise you?
you know what clothes cost?
what food costs?
you just sit in your damned
room moping on your
dead ass!
16 years old and you act
like a dead man!
what are ya gonna do when
you get out in the world?
look at Benny Halsey, he's
an usher in a
theater!
Billy Evans sells newspapers
on the corner of Crenshaw
and Olympic
and you say you can't
find a job!
well, the truth is, you just
don't want a job!
I got a job!

anybody who really wants a
job can get a job!
I got a good god damned
mind to throw you out on the
street,
all you do is sit around and
mope!
I can't believe you're my
son!
your mother is ashamed
of you!
you're killing your mother!
I got a good mind to beat
the shit out of you, just to
wake you up!
what?
don't talk to me like that!
I'M YOUR FATHER!
DON'T EVER TALK TO
ME LIKE THAT AGAIN!
WHAT?
ALL RIGHT, ALL RIGHT,
OUT OF THIS HOUSE!
YOU'RE OUT!
OUT!
OUT!
MAMA, I'M THROWING
THIS SON OF A
BITCH OUT!

MAMA!

1/2/93 8:43 PM

Dear *New York Quarterly*:

I am a native Albino who lives with a mother with a wooden
leg and a father who shoots up. I have a parrot, Cagney, who
says, "Yankee Doodle Dandy!" each time he excretes, which is
4 or 5 times a day. I once saw J. D. Salinger. Enclosed are my
Flying Saucer Poems. I have an 18-year-old sister with a body
like you've never seen. Nude photos enclosed. In case my
poems are rejected, these photos are to be returned. In case of
acceptance, I or my sister can be reached at 642-696-6969.

sincerely yours,
Byron Keats

musings

the temple of my doorway is
locked.

I only agree with my critics when they are
wrong.

my father was blind in one eye, deaf in one ear
and wrong in one life.

United States postage stamps are the ugliest
in the world.

Hemingway's characters were consistently
grim, which meant they tried too
hard.

mornings are the worst, noons are a little
better and the nights are best.
by the time you are ready to sleep you
are feeling best of all.

constant sewage spills just strengthen my
convictions.

the best thing about Immanuel Kant was
his name.

to live well is a matter of definition.

God is an invention of Man; Woman, of the
Devil.

only boring people get bored.

lonely people are avoided because they are
lonely and they are lonely because they are
avoided.

people who prefer to be alone have some
damn good reasons for it.

people who prefer to be alone and lonely people
cannot be put in the same room together.

if you tape a coconut to your ass under your pants,
you can walk around like that for two weeks before
anybody asks you about that.

the best book is the one you've never read; the
best woman, the one you've never met.

if man were meant to fly he would have been
born with wings attached to his body.
I'll admit that I have flown without them but it's
an unnatural act, that's why I keep asking the
stewardess for drinks.

if you sit in a dark room for some months you'll
have some wonderful thoughts before you go
crazy.

there is hardly anything as sad as a run-over
cat.

the basis of Capitalism is to sell something for
far more than its worth.
the more you can do this, the richer you can
become.
everybody screws somebody else in a different
kind of way.
I screw you by writing words.

bliss only means forgetting for a while what is
to come.

Hell never stops it only pauses.

this is a pause.

enjoy it while you can.

storm for the living and the dead

you can't beat me, the rain is coming through
the door and I'm at this computer while
listening to Rachmaninov on the radio,
the rain is coming right through the door,
flicks of it and I blow cigar smoke at it and
smile.
outside the door is a little balcony and there
is a chair there.
I sometimes sit in that chair when things go
bad here.
(damn the rain is coming down now!
great! beating down on my wooden chair
out there!
the trees are shaking in the rain and the
phone wires.)

I sometimes sit in that chair when things
go bad
and I drink beer out there,
watch the cars of night on the freeway,
also notice how many lights are needed
in a city, so many.
and I sit there and think, well, it may
be a down time

but at least you're not on skid row.
you're not even in the graveyard yet.
buck up, old boy, you've fought past
worse than this . . .
drink your beer.

but tonight I'm in here,
and Rachmaninov still plays for me.
when I was a young man in San
Francisco, or fairly young, I was
a bit mentally unbalanced, I thought
I was a great artist and I starved for
it.
what I mean is, Rachmaninov was
still alive then
and somehow I had saved enough
money to go see him play at the
auditorium.
only when I got in there it was
announced that he was ill
and that a replacement would
play for him.
this made me angry.
I shouldn't have been for within
a week he was
dead.
but he's playing for me now.
one of his own compositions,
and doing very well.
as the rain flicks into this room,
now a gale-like wind blows the
door totally open.

papers fly about the room.

there is a knock on the door,
the door behind me.
it opens.
my wife comes in.

"it's a hurricane!" she says,
"an icy one, you'll freeze to
death!"

"no, no," I tell her, "I'm fine!"

she feels my arms,
they are warm.

she stands staring at me.
sometimes she wonders.
so do I.

now I am alone.
Rachmaninov has finished,
and the rain has
stopped.
and the wind.

now I'm cold.

I get up and put on a bathrobe.

I'm an old writer.

a phone bill looks at me
upside down.

the party is over.
San Pedro, 1993,
in the Lord of our
Year.

sitting here.

cover charge

Doug and I had a table up front,
one of the best, the girls were
kicking their legs high, the music
was good and the drinks were
coming.
but right in the middle of it I
saw something go by.
oh oh, I thought, that was my
death, I just saw my death go
by.
"I just saw my death go by," I
told Doug.
"what?" he asked, "I can't hear
you!"
"DEATH!" I screamed.
"forget it," he said, "drink up!"

when the set was over, one of
the girls, Mandy, Doug knew
her, came over and sat down.
her head was the head of
Death.
"why are you staring at me?"
she asked.

"you remind me of something,"
I said.
"what?" she asked.
I just smiled.
"I gotta go," she said.

"you scared her off," said
Doug.
"she scared me," I said.
then I looked at Doug.
his head was the head of
Death.
he didn't know it, only I
knew it.
"what the hell you looking
at?" he asked me.
"nothing," I told him.
"you look like you saw a
ghost," he said, "you sick
or something?"
"I'm fine, Doug."
"well, Jesus, I mean we
spend all this money to
have a ball and you act
like you're at a
funeral."

then the comedian came
on, a big fat guy with a
paper hat, he blew a
whistle and pulled a
balloon out of his butt

and said something that
I couldn't quite hear
and everybody laughed
and laughed.
I couldn't laugh.
I saw my death walk by.
it was the waiter.
I signaled him over to
order a drink.
all at once he turned into
this hard steel ball
and he came roaring at
me with the speed of a
bullet as I shot up
ripping the table over,
the light shattered.
some people laughed
and some screamed.

"YOU REMIND ME OF SOMETHING," I SAID.

good stuff

sucking on this cigar,
drinking bottle after bottle of beer from
the people's Republic of
China,
it's early in the dark morning
and I am celebrating the existence of
all of us,
all of us rag-headed, doom-sucking
inhabitants of this monstrous
dung ball of
earth.
I tell you, all, one and all, that I am
proud of you
for not cutting your throats each
morning as you rise to meet it
again.
of course, some of you do, you screw
off, get out and leave us with the
stinking after-fall, leave us to handle
the mangled, the half-murdered, the
incompetent, the mad, the vile, the
masses.

but I blow blue smoke and suck on
these green bottles
in celebration of those who remain,
in whatever fashion, muddled and
incongruous but holding,
the pitcher who blazes in the bean
ball at 97 m.p.h.
the bus driver grinding his gums raw
while staying on schedule.
the wetbacks who awaken me at
7 A.M. with their leaf-blowers.
your mother, somebody's mother,
your son, somebody's son, some
sister, some cousin, some old fart
in a walker, all there.
look't 'em.

I salute those who retain the treacher-
ous grip.
I open a new green bottle, flick my
dead cigar back to life with a yellow
lighter.
we need the people to clean our
latrines.
we need the mercy of breathing,
moving life
even if most of it is
incontinent.

beer from China,
think of it.
this is some A.M.
Caesar and Plato hulk in the
shadows and I love you all
for just a
moment.

now

rife; tear off the label;
the big guns have been
lowered.
nothing to do now but
sit in the sun
and ponder how you got
from the past to the
present.
now you know . . . what? that
there was nothing so special
about you
after all.
you kept getting into fights
where you didn't
belong, you were in over your
head.
you should have eased off
more.
you took on too much and they
burned you—
too much drink, too many women,
too many books.
it didn't matter all that much.
now you watch the minutes run

up your arms.
you hear dogs bark.
you're tired enough to listen
now.
you're an old man in a chair
in a yard
in the world.
a leaf drops on your white belly
and that's all there
is.

quit before the sun

turn left at Moscow or
meet me at the *Enchilada House*.

the dogs have dragged me this
far.
I am numbed by Fate
but game as a linebacker in the
4th quarter.

drink?
or think?
better drink.

we have become the philosopher
of stone
for want of better things.
we used to destroy, now we note
what remains:
us, them, we and the
machinery.
neatly bound like the snail and
the leaf.
what god awful gaff these rules
are!
who set this up?
get the bastard, roast him with the

lamb!
fun to say, what?
like Mary had a little lamb and left
town on the
9:15.
stone stuff.
stern stuff, with a downward
smile.

drink?
doesn't matter,
and it does.

what matters most is what happens to
somebody else, not
yourself.
how odd it would come down to
this.
alpine spring water couldn't say it
better.
or the ten count.

the unexpected magic of a point
well made
can get you from fire to fire,
from hell to hell.
that's what it's all about, there on
the side of the
stone.
turn left at Moscow, come down
from Denver.

drink.

#I

---

oh, forgive me For Whom the Bell Tolls,
oh, forgive me Man who walked on water,
oh, forgive me little old woman who lived in a shoe,
oh, forgive me the mountain that roared at midnight,
oh, forgive me the dumb sounds of night and day and death,
oh, forgive me the death of the last beautiful panther,
oh, forgive me all the sunken ships and defeated armies,
this is my first FAX POEM.
it's too late:
I have been
smitten.

song for this softly-sweeping sorrow ...

one must arise
above all this shit,
keep growing ...
destiny is only a whore if we make her
so.
let's light lights
let's suffer in the grand style—
toothpick in mouth, grinning.
we can do it.
we were born strong and we will die
strong.
the manner of our living
like ocean liners in the fog ...
thorns on roses ...
blasé boys trotting the parks in swim suits ...
it has been very
good.
our bones
like stems into the sky
will forever cry
victory.

sources

"caught again at some impossible pass." c. 1959 manuscript; previously
    unpublished.
"in this—" c. 1960 manuscript; previously unpublished.
"prayer for broken-handed lovers." *Quicksilver* 13.3, Autumn 1960; previously
    uncollected.
"why are all your poems personal?" *Wanderlust* 10, April 1961; previously
    uncollected.
"fast pace." *Brand "X"* 1, January 1962; previously uncollected.
"I think of Hemingway." (April 1962); *El Corno Emplumado* 7, July 1963;
    previously uncollected.
"I was shit." c. late 1962 manuscript; previously unpublished.
"corrections of self, mostly after Whitman:" *Signet* 5.1, January 1963;
    previously uncollected.
"the bumblebee." Early 1963 manuscript; previously unpublished.
"warble in." *Coastlines* 20, 1963; previously uncollected.
"a trainride in hell." (May 1963); *Evidence* 9, late 1965; previously uncollected.
"same old thing, Shakespeare through Mailer—" *Wormwood Review* 11,
    November 1963; previously uncollected.
"the rope of glass." August 1964 manuscript; previously unpublished.
"tough luck." c. late 1966 manuscript; previously unpublished.
"sometimes when I feel blue I listen to Mahler." *Kauri* 18, January-February
    1967; previously uncollected.
"men's crapper." *Intrepid* 7, March 1967; based on an earlier, unpublished draft
    titled "the human inhuman"; previously uncollected.
"like a flyswatter." Early 1968 manuscript; previously uncollected.
"take me out to the ball game." August 20, 1968 manuscript; based on an earlier,
    unpublished draft titled "song of the vanquished"; previously uncollected.
"I thought I was going to get some." *Laugh Literary and Man the Humping
    Guns* 1, May 1969; previously uncollected.
"charity ward." *Planet* 1.5, July 1969; based on an earlier, unpublished draft
    titled "good service, at last"; previously uncollected.
"like that." (Late 1969); *Lemming* 1, Winter 1971; previously uncollected.
"phone call from my 5-year-old daughter in Garden Grove." c. early 1970
    manuscript; previously unpublished.

"the solar mass: soul: genesis and geotropism:" c. 1970 manuscript; previously unpublished.

"hooked on horse." *Heads Up* 5, 1970; previously uncollected.

"fuck." c. 1970 manuscript; previously unpublished.

"2 immortal poems." c. 1970 manuscript; previously unpublished.

"T.H.I.A.L.H." c. 1970 manuscript (second draft); previously unpublished.

"the lesbian." *Statement* 27, May 1970; previously uncollected.

"a poem to myself." (c. 1970); *Something Else Yearbook,* 1973; previously uncollected.

"fact." (October 1970); *Buffalo Stamps* 1.2, 1971; previously uncollected.

"blues song." *Epos* 22.2; Winter 1970–71; previously uncollected.

"fat upon the land." *Vagabond* 10, early 1971; previously uncollected.

"love song." March 1971 manuscript; previously uncollected.

"poem for Dante." *Second Aeon* 13, 1971; previously uncollected.

"the conditions." c. 1971 manuscript; previously uncollected.

"29 chilled grapes." July 17, 1971 manuscript; previously uncollected.

"burning in water, drowning in flame." November 19, 1971 manuscript; previously uncollected.

"a cop-out to a possible immortality:" October 8, 1972 manuscript; previously uncollected.

"well, now that Ezra has died . . . " (November 1972); *Choice* 9, 1974; previously uncollected.

"warts." October 7, 1973 manuscript; previously uncollected.

"my new parents." December 4, 1973 manuscript; previously uncollected.

"something about the action:" c. 1973 manuscript; previously unpublished.

"55 beds in the same direction." *Wormwood Review* 53, early 1974; previously uncollected.

"b." January 20, 1975 manuscript; previously uncollected.

"finger." January 20, 1975 manuscript; previously unpublished.

"the thing." April 15, 1975 manuscript; previously unpublished.

"Bob Dylan." December 3, 1975 manuscript; previously uncollected.

"Texsun." December 14, 1975 manuscript; previously uncollected.

"warm water bubbles." c. 1975 manuscript; previously unpublished.

"a corny poem." January 23, 1976 manuscript; previously unpublished.

"the ladies of the afternoon." *Black Moss* 2.2, Fall 1976; previously uncollected.

"tongue-cut." November 13, 1977 manuscript; previously uncollected.

"Venice, Calif., nov. 1977:" November 29, 1977 manuscript; previously unpublished.

"mirror." February 4, 1978 manuscript; previously uncollected.

"head jobs." *The Apalachee Quarterly* 11, Summer 1978; based on an earlier draft written on June 17, 1978; previously uncollected.

"chili and beans." August 26, 1979 manuscript; based on an earlier, unpublished draft titled "to the drunks along the bar before closing time"; previously uncollected.

"go to your grave cleanly—" c. 1979 manuscript; previously unpublished.

"kuv stuff mox out." *Orpheus* 1, Spring 1980; based on an earlier draft written on May 8, 1978; previously uncollected.

"a long hot day at the track." *Scree* 17/18, 1981; based on an earlier draft written on July 16, 1978; previously uncollected.

"the letters of John Steinbeck." *Bachy* 18, 1981; based on an earlier draft written on July 21, 1978; previously uncollected.

"and the trivial lives of royalty never excited me either . . ." November 17, 1981 manuscript; previously uncollected.

"letter to a friend with a domestic problem:" December 26, 1981 manuscript; previously uncollected.

"agnostic." January 26, 1982 manuscript; previously uncollected.

"clones." February 17, 1982 manuscript; previously unpublished.

"gnawed by dull crisis." *Poetry/LA* 4, Spring-Summer 1982; previously uncollected.

"I been working on the railroad . . ." December 28, 1982 manuscript; previously uncollected.

"the way it goes." May 18, 1983 manuscript; previously unpublished.

"alone in a time of armies." July 17, 1984 manuscript; previously uncollected.

"going modern." *Oro Madre* 10, 1984; based on an earlier draft written on September 12, 1984; previously uncollected.

"it doesn't always work." (c. Summer 1985); *New York Quarterly* 29, Spring 1986; previously uncollected.

"I have this room." (June 1985); *Wormwood Review* 141, 1996; previously uncollected.

"a man for the centuries." (October 1985); *Second Coming* 14.1, 1986; previously uncollected.

"dear old dad." June 18, 1986 manuscript; previously uncollected.

"peace and love." *New York Quarterly* 31, Fall 1986; previously uncollected.

"the world of valets." *Second Coming* 16.2, late 1986; previously uncollected.

"I live to write and now I'm dying." *Scream* 5, 1987; previously uncollected.

"rip it." *Once More With Feeling*, 1988; previously uncollected.

"Henry Miller and Burroughs." c. 1988 manuscript; previously uncollected.

"family tree." *Poetry/LA* 17, Fall-Winter 1988–89; previously uncollected.

"being here." *Poetry/LA* 18, Spring-Summer 1989; previously uncollected.

"the only life." December 16, 1989 manuscript; previously uncollected.

"stomping at the Savoy." March 4, 1990 manuscript; previously unpublished.

"the glory days." June 18, 1990 manuscript; previously uncollected.

A TIMELESS SELECTION OF SOME OF CHARLES BUKOWSKI'S
BEST UNPUBLISHED AND UNCOLLECTED POEMS

Charles Bukowski was a prolific writer who produced countless short stories, novels, and poems that have reached beyond their time and place to speak to generations of readers all over the world. Many of his poems remain little known since they appeared in small magazines but were never collected, and a large number of them have yet to be published.

In *Storm for the Living and the Dead,* Abel Debritto has curated a collection of rare and never-before-seen material—poems from obscure, hard-to-find magazines, as well as from libraries and private collections all over the country. In doing so, Debritto has captured the essence of Bukowski's inimitable poetic style—tough and hilarious but ringing with humanity. *Storm for the Living and the Dead* is a gift for any devotee of the Dirty Old Man of American letters.

CHARLES BUKOWSKI is one of America's best-known contemporary writers of poetry and prose and, many would claim, its most influential and imitated poet. He was born in 1920 in Andernach, Germany, to an American soldier father and a German mother, and brought to the United States at the age of two. He was raised in Los Angeles and lived there for more than fifty years. He died in San Pedro, California, on March 9, 1994, at the age of seventy-three, shortly after completing his last novel, *Pulp.*

ABEL DEBRITTO, a former Fulbright scholar and current Marie Curie scholar, works in the digital humanities. He is the author of *Charles Bukowski, King of the Underground,* and the editor of the Bukowski collections *On Writing, On Cats,* and *On Love.*

ecco
An Imprint of HarperCollinsPublishers

Available from HarperCollins e-books

Cover design by Sara Wood
Cover photograph © Ulf Andersen/Getty Images
Author photograph © Michael Montfort

ISBN 978-0-06-265652-0

51800

9 780062 656520

EAN

USA $18.00 / CAN $22.00

0119